SAGE Study Skills

Good Essay Writing

A Social Sciences Guide

Fifth Edition

Peter Redman & Wendy Maples

The Open University

 SAGE

Los Angeles | London | New Delhi
Singapore | Washington DC | Melbourne

Los Angeles | London | New Delhi
Singapore | Washington DC | Melbourne

SAGE Publications Ltd
1 Oliver's Yard
55 City Road
London EC1Y 1SP

SAGE Publications Inc.
2455 Teller Road
Thousand Oaks, California 91320

SAGE Publications India Pvt Ltd
B 1/I 1 Mohan Cooperative Industrial Area
Mathura Road
New Delhi 110 044

SAGE Publications Asia-Pacific Pte Ltd
3 Church Street
#10-04 Samsung Hub
Singapore 049483

Editor: Marianne Lagrange
Editorial assistant: Rob Patterson
Production editor: Tom Bedford
Copyeditor: Aud Scriven
Proofreader: Andy Baxter
Indexer: Cathy Heath
Marketing manager: Catherine Slinn
Cover design: Sheila Tong
Typeset by: C&M Digitals (P) Ltd, Chennai, India
Printed by: CPI Group (UK) Ltd, Croydon, CR0 4YY

© Peter Redman and Wendy Maples 2017

First edition published by the Open University 1998.
Second edition published in 2001 and reprinted in 2004
(twice) and 2005, third edition published in 2005 and
reprinted in 2006, 2007, 2008 and 2009, fourth edition
published in 2011 and reprinted in 2015 and 2016.

This fifth edition first published 2017.

Library of Congress Control Number: 2016947109

British Library Cataloguing in Publication data

A catalogue record for this book is available from
the British Library

ISBN 978-1-4739-8217-8
ISBN 978-1-4739-8216-1 (pbk)

Good Essay Writing

Sara Miller McCune founded SAGE Publishing in 1965 to support the dissemination of usable knowledge and educate a global community. SAGE publishes more than 1000 journals and over 800 new books each year, spanning a wide range of subject areas. Our growing selection of library products includes archives, data, case studies and video. SAGE remains majority owned by our founder and after her lifetime will become owned by a charitable trust that secures the company's continued independence.

Los Angeles | London | New Delhi | Singapore | Washington DC | Melbourne

Contents

About the Authors   viii

Preface and Acknowledgements to the Fifth Edition   ix

Companion Website   xi

1 Introduction   1

  1.1 How to use this guide   2
  1.2 Will the guide tell you everything about essay writing?   4

2 What Is a Social Science Essay?   6

  2.1 The structure of a basic social science essay   6
  2.2 What is distinctive about a social science essay?   7
  2.3 Common errors in essays   10
  2.4 Four golden rules for writing a social science essay   12

3 Stages of Writing, from Preparation to Final Version   14

  3.1 Read the question and any essay guidance notes   15
  3.2 Use feedback   16
  3.3 Identify and organize the relevant material:
            drafting an essay plan   18
  3.4 First draft to final version   21
  3.5 Time management   22

4 Matching the Answer to the Question   24

  4.1 Unpacking the question   24
  4.2 Command words and cognitive skills   25
  4.3 Types of social science essay questions   31

5 Reading, Note-taking and Literature Searches   38

    5.1 Reading   38
    5.2 Taking notes   45
    5.3 Academic literature searches and gathering data   49

6 Thinking Critically and Formulating an Argument   55

    6.1 Critical thinking   55
    6.2 Formulating an argument   58

7 Writing Introductions   61

    7.1 Longer or 'full' introductions   62
    7.2 Basic short introductions   66
    7.3 When do you write the introduction?   67

8 Writing the Main Section   69

    8.1 Structuring your argument   69
    8.2 Using evidence to support your argument   72
    8.3 Adding weight to your argument   84
    8.4 Communicating your argument   87

9 Writing Conclusions   95

    9.1 What a conclusion should aim to do – and should not do 95
    9.2 What a conclusion should contain   96

10 Referencing   99

    10.1 What is a reference?   99
    10.2 Why are references needed?   100
    10.3 What should be referenced?   101
    10.4 Basic principles   101
    10.5 Advanced referencing   115
    10.6 Compiling your references   118

11 Essay-writing Skills and Other Forms of Social
     Science Writing   121

    11.1 Academic essays and other critical writing   121
    11.2 Why an essay is not a news article or a report   122
    11.3 Using essay-writing skills in other forms
           of written assessment   123

12 Some Common Worries   127

12.1   Writing too much or too little   127
12.2   Using the 'I' word, 'subjectivity' and 'objectivity'   128
12.3   Using your own experience   129
12.4   Presentation, spelling, grammar and punctuation   129
12.5   Plagiarism and poor academic practice   130

13 What Tutors Look for When Marking Essays   136

13.1   Marking schemes: criteria related to grade bands   137
13.2   Writing skills: 'introductory', 'intermediate'
       and 'advanced' essays   140

14 Examples of Student Essays   146

Essay 1   147
Essay 2   155
Essay 3   160
Essay 4   166

*Appendix A: Editors' Symbols – Common Notations
Made by Tutors*   173

*Appendix B: Abbreviations and Words in
Foreign Languages*   175

References   177

Index   179

About the Authors

Peter Redman has been teaching social science at The Open University for the last twenty-five years. During this time he has worked closely with numerous students, helping them reflect on and improve their writing skills. He is a Senior Lecturer in Sociology.

Wendy Maples has been teaching in higher education for over twenty-five years. She has worked on a number of interdisciplinary courses for The Open University, writing course texts on social science research methods and environment, as well as creating learning development materials for students and teaching development materials for lecturers. Dr Maples is a Senior Fellow of the Higher Education Academy.

Preface and Acknowledgements to the Fifth Edition

Previous editions of *Good Essay Writing* have aimed to provide practical and easily accessible advice on writing social science essays. The fifth edition continues in this vein but offers, in addition to a redesigned and updated text, specifically new material – in particular making best use of online sources and more examples of different forms of essay style writing. The accompanying website (https://study.sagepub.com/redmanandmaples5) has also been revised and expanded.

Good Essay Writing is the outcome of a series of collective efforts. Some of the best ideas to be found in the guide came from a team of Open University Associate Lecturers who commented on and contributed to the early drafts of *Good Essay Writing*'s first incarnation. They were Sue Cole, Rosie Collins, Rick Davies, Peter Hull, Mary Larkin, Liz Ockleford, Isobel Shelton and Andy Sutton. Chris Brook, Ross Fergusson, Chris Nichols, Diane Watson and Helen Wescott contributed additional material to the first edition and the second edition incorporated further ideas from Geraldine Carpenter, Vicki Goodwin, Mary Langan, Janet MacDonald and Alison Rolfe. Much of the companion website material that accompanied the redesigned fourth edition was conceived of and written by Rob Parsons. Much of the material from previous editions reappears here and our thanks are therefore due to all of these people.

This fifth edition owes further debts of gratitude to Wal Evans, Stephen Henderson, Rob Parsons and Colette Ankers De Salis, who offered support in locating new authentic student material. We also owe sincere thanks to Open University students Evie Beattie; Louise Chalmers-Stevens, Louise Diez, Phil Ellis; Teresa Garrard; Hazel Hart; David Knight; Abbie Krovena, Katie Palmer, Emma Percy, Alex Pollard and David Purcell, whose essays or essay extracts were selected to appear in the book or on the website. Special mention should also go to Jonathan Davies, who designed the first edition, and to Peggotty Graham, who supported the original Open University project.

While these contributions proved invaluable, this and previous editions of the guide owe a particular debt of gratitude to two further people. The first is Helen Lentell, who had the original idea for *Good Essay Writing*, put together the initial project team and contributed much to the Guide's first edition. The second is Lynne Slocombe, who not only edited the first and second editions but also provided much of the material on referencing which reappears here.

Companion Website

Good Essay Writing is supported by a wealth of online resources for both students and lecturers to aid study and support teaching, which are available at https://study.sagepub.com/redmanandmaples5

For students

- **Additional student essay examples** and related tasks to help you structure your essays
- **Interactive click & reveal tasks** ask you to unshuffle jumbled references and reveal tutor comments to contrast and compare with your own assessments
- **Downloadable and editable summary sheets** to help you plan how to approach your next assignment
- **Many more resources and exercises to help progress your essay writing skills!**

1

Introduction

- How to use this guide
- Will the guide tell you everything about essay writing?

Many students, however experienced, find essay writing difficult. There is, of course, no guaranteed recipe, no absolute method for producing a good essay. However, it is the purpose of this book to recommend and illustrate proven approaches and techniques which, combined with practice, will increase your confidence and skill and thereby improve the quality and effectiveness of your academic writing.

Throughout the book you will find examples of good practice that will help you in this task. These include how to 'wordstorm' your initial ideas, organize and plan your essay, write effective introductions and conclusions, build an effective argument, use evidence, and provide accurate references. Summary sections will help to reinforce your understanding of these issues, while extracts from academic texts and real, sample essays further illustrate the points being made. These all serve to demonstrate how your initial ideas can be transformed into the clear, flowing prose of a well-written essay.

As *Good Essay Writing* has been written by Open University (OU) or former OU academics, you may find terms that are common in the OU but are less common in your home university. For instance, we use the term 'tutor' to describe the person leading teaching on a course – or module – and who is responsible for marking and assessing your essays. In other universities the terms 'lecturer' or 'professor' might be more readily used.

As the book is published in the UK, there are some (minor) writing conventions that may be unfamiliar to you if you are reading this elsewhere in the world. For instance, in the USA, punctuation following a quotation that ends a sentence looks like this:

> Megan Poore (2014) tells students to 'never be afraid … to find new ways of doing things.'

The full stop, or period, is *inside* the quotation mark, or inverted comma.
In this book, you will see this punctuation convention instead:

> Megan Poore (2014) tells students to 'never be afraid … to find new ways of doing things'.

Placing the full stop at the end of the sentence, rather than the end of the quote, is the convention in the UK. A grammar dictionary can help you with such details.
You will also find that we use 'social science' as a broad generic term which includes subjects such as sociology, politics, geography, psychology, social policy and economics. However, there are many other subject areas where students are required to produce 'social science' essays. For this reason the book and its accompanying website include sample material from business, health and social care, environment and education.
In brief, the guide aims to:

- introduce key essay-writing skills and accepted conventions in the social sciences;
- recap on social science essay-writing skills for those who have already done some studies in the social sciences or related areas;
- introduce more advanced essay-writing skills.

If your aim is to write better essays, and you want quick, practical advice and guidance that draws on years of successful and high-quality teaching, then *Good Essay Writing* is for you.

1.1 How to use this guide

Inevitably, some readers will be familiar with much of the material in *Good Essay Writing*. However, some aspects may be new to you, and other parts will help you build on or develop what you already know. As such, you should view *Good Essay Writing* as a resource that you can adapt to your own needs.

The chapters that follow cover the main aspects of essay writing, ending with 'Summaries' of some general points to look out for and 'self-test' questions to consolidate your reading.

Chapters 2–6 provide an outline of the characteristics of social science essays; demonstrate some of the essential study skills you will need to prepare for essay writing; explore some basic principles of essay writing; provide recommendations on how to approach different types of essay questions; and discuss planning and preparation.

Chapter 7 looks specifically at forming and shaping an introduction.

Chapter 8 looks at writing the main section of a social science essay, exploring how to structure an argument, how to support your case with evidence, and how to communicate your argument effectively.

Chapter 9 discusses conclusion writing.

Chapter 10 explains how to compile references.

Chapter 11 considers the similarities and differences between formal social science essays and other common written formats, and the use of essay-writing skills in other written assessments.

Chapter 12 looks at some common worries that people have about writing essays.

Chapter 13 considers what tutors look for in introductory level, intermediate and advanced essays, and describes common indicators of performance by grade band.

Chapter 14 consists of four examples of full student essays and comments by tutors on the essays' strengths and weaknesses.

Finally, there are two Appendices.

Appendix A lists common editors' notations used by tutors which you may find in feedback on your essays.

Appendix B explains abbreviations and words in foreign languages that are commonly found in English academic writing.

How can you use the guide most effectively?

There are several approaches (as you can see from the bullet points below), and it will probably be best if you combine them to produce a strategy that works for you. You might decide to:

- read *Good Essay Writing* from cover to cover;
- skim-read sections that you already know enough about;
- work systematically through individual chapters such as 'Writing the main section';
- concentrate on the Summaries and prompt questions at the end of each chapter;
- use the Contents pages and Index to pinpoint particular issues that are relevant to you and ignore the rest;

- use *Good Essay Writing* as a 'reference' book, returning to it whenever you need to look up something or remind yourself of a particular point;
- use some sections as reference material; for example, the Appendix on common markers' notations.

1.2 Will the guide tell you everything about essay writing?

Good Essay Writing is a quick guide designed to help you build on your essay-writing skills and improve your abilities to communicate effectively as a social scientist. It is not intended to – nor could it – provide all the detailed guidance that you may need for each and every course that you study. Nor does it cover more specialized tasks, such as project writing, or how to configure graphs and tables and so on. Similarly, it is not intended as an extended, interactive course in essay writing. Its intention is to be short, practical and easily accessible.

As a result, the Guide cannot promise to transform your essay writing overnight. The truth is that there is no magic formula that will guarantee you a good grade for every essay that you produce. In fact, there is no one 'correct' way to write an essay. Sometimes the most exciting essays will be those that address a question in an unexpected way, that challenge its fundamental premises, or that succeed in producing new insights rather than recycling well-worn ideas. The advice in this guide suggests some generally agreed conventions, but these are not the only ones available and they do not by themselves add up to a great essay.

Your essay writing will improve mainly as a result of your own hard work in thinking things through for yourself, through experience, and through your increasing knowledge of the fields in which you work. The advice you find in *Good Essay Writing* should be used in tandem with the advice you get from your course or module tutor. This advice may be offered in your tutorials or at lectures, or as written feedback on your essays. Written feedback can be invaluable, which is why one of the bits of advice offered in *Good Essay Writing* is to read carefully any comments offered by your tutor. You may also have online resources at your university to support study skills, including essay writing. In addition to this, Sage, the publishers of this book, have provided a companion website (https://study.sagepub.com/redmanandmaples5) that you can access which includes additional materials specifically for use with *Good Essay Writing*. Here you will find a series of activities and downloads, additional sample essays with tutor comments, and further guidance on note-taking and referencing. There are also some self-help activities to help you develop good practice and identify areas where you might need further revision. You will find linked activities or downloads on the website when you see this symbol (in the margin to the right) at the beginning of the relevant section.

'How to' guides like this one are rather like cookery books: they can tell you what the ingredients are, and they can suggest ways to mix the ingredients together. What they cannot do is turn you into a gourmet chef. Like cooking, essay writing is not something you ever stop learning about. However, the advice in *Good Essay Writing* should help you become more confident and more creative in your work and, in so doing, improve the overall quality of your writing.

Self-test

1   How have you approached reading this book? Have you read the Table of Contents? Have you scanned through the chapters?
2   How do you intend to proceed? Do you have a plan for using the book?
3   Do you have a sense of your own essay-writing and structuring skills?

Don't forget! Visit https://study.sagepub.com/redmanandmaples5 for more tasks and resources related to this chapter.

2

What Is a Social Science Essay?

- The structure of a basic social science essay
- What is distinctive about a social science essay?
- Common errors in essays
- Four golden rules for writing a social science essay

In this chapter we consider what is distinctive about essay writing and, in particular, essay writing in the social sciences. To start with, we look at the structure of social science essays.

2.1 The structure of a basic social science essay

There are various types of social science essay, and essays of different lengths require slightly different approaches (this will be addressed later). However, all social science essays share a basic structure which is common to many academic subject areas. At its simplest, a social science essay looks something like this:

- *Title:* Every essay should begin with the title written out in full. In some cases this will simply be the set question or statement for discussion.
- *Introduction:* The introduction tells the reader what the essay is about.
- *Main section:* The main section, or 'body', of the essay develops the key points of the argument in a 'logical progression'. It uses evidence from research (empirical evidence) and theoretical arguments to support those points.

- *Conclusion:* The conclusion reassesses the arguments presented in the main section in order to make a final statement in answer to the question.
- *List of references:* This provides full details of the publications referred to in the text.

2.2 What is distinctive about a social science essay?

As you are no doubt aware, essay writing is a common feature of undergraduate study in many different subjects. What, then, is distinctive about essay writing in the social sciences? There are particular features that characterize social science essays, and that relate to what is called the *epistemological* underpinning of work in this area (that is, to ideas about what constitutes valid social scientific knowledge and where this comes from). Among the most important of these characteristics are:

- the requirement that you support arguments with *evidence,* particularly evidence that is the product of systematic and rigorous research (see sections 5.3, 6.1 and 8.2);
- the use of *theory* to build explanations about how the social world works (see section 8.2).

Evidence is important in social scientific writing because it is used to support or query beliefs, propositions or hypotheses about the social world. Let's take an example. A social scientist may ask: 'Does prison work?'. This forms an initial *question*, but one that is too vague to explore as it stands. (This question might be about whether prison 'works' for offenders, in terms of providing rehabilitation, or re-education; or it might be about whether it 'works' for victims of crime who may wish to see retribution – or any number of other issues.) To answer the question in mind, the social scientist will need to formulate a more specific *claim* (or *hypothesis),* one that can be systematically and rigorously explored. Such a claim could be formulated in the following terms: 'Imprisonment reduces the likelihood of subsequent reoffending'. This claim can now be subjected to systematic research. In other words, the social scientist will gather *evidence* for and against this claim, evidence that she or he will then interpret or *evaluate.* This process of evaluation will seek to support or refute the original claim, but it may be inconclusive, and/or it may generate further questions. Together, these processes of enquiry can be described as forming a 'circuit of social scientific knowledge'. This circuit can be represented as shown in Figure 2.1.

Undergraduates may sometimes be asked to conduct their own small-scale research, for instance a time-limited observation, a small number of interviews, or some content analysis. However, the focus of social science study at

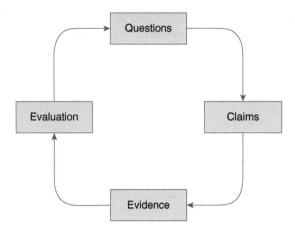

Figure 2.1 The circuit of social scientific knowledge

Sherratt et al., 2000, p. 18.

undergraduate level, and particularly in the first two years of study, will be largely on the research of others. Generally, in preparing for writing your essays, the expectation will be that you will identify and evaluate evidence from existing research. However, the principle holds good: in writing social science essays you will need to find evidence for and against any claim, and you will need to evaluate that evidence.

Theory is important in social scientific writing because the theoretical orientation of the social scientist will tend to inform the types of question she or he asks, the specific claims tested, the ways in which evidence is identified and gathered, and the manner in which this evidence is interpreted and evaluated. In other words, the theoretical orientation of the social scientist is liable to impact upon the forms of knowledge she or he will produce.

Take, for example, the research question we asked above: 'Does prison work?'. A pragmatic, policy-oriented social scientist may seek to answer this question by formulating a specific claim of the sort we identified, 'Imprisonment reduces the likelihood of reoffending'. She or he may then gather evidence of reoffending rates among matched groups of convicted criminals, comparing those who were imprisoned with those who were given an alternative punishment, such as forms of community service. Evidence that imprisonment did not produce significantly lower rates of reoffending than community service may then be interpreted as suggesting that prison does not work, or that it works only up to a point. However, another social scientist might look at the same research findings and come to a different conclusion, perhaps that the apparent failure of prison to reduce reoffending demonstrates that its primary purpose lies elsewhere. Indeed, more 'critically' oriented social scientists (for example, those informed by Marxism or the work of Michel Foucault) have sought to argue that the growth of prisons in the nineteenth century was part of wider social attempts to 'discipline' specific populations, in particular, the working class.

The issue here is not whether these more 'critical' arguments are right or wrong but that a social scientist's theoretical orientation will inform how she or he evaluates the available evidence. In fact, it is likely that a 'critical' social scientist of this sort would have formulated a different research 'claim'. For example, rather than seeking to test the claim, 'Imprisonment reduces the likelihood of reoffending', the critical social scientist might have sought to test the proposition, 'Prisons are part of wider social strategies that aim to produce "disciplined" subjects'. The point for you to take away from this discussion is, then, that the theories we use shape the forms of social scientific knowledge we produce (see Figure 2.2).

There is considerable debate within the social sciences about the exact relationship between theory and evidence. To simplify somewhat, some social scientists tend to argue that evidence can be used to support or invalidate the claims investigated by researchers and thereby produce theoretical accounts of the social world that are more or less accurate. Other social scientists will tend to argue that our theoretical orientations (and the value judgements and taken-for-granted assumptions that they contain) shape the processes of social scientific enquiry itself, such that we can never claim to produce a straightforwardly 'accurate' account of the social world. Instead, they suggest that social scientific knowledge is always produced from a particular standpoint and will inevitably reflect its assumptions.

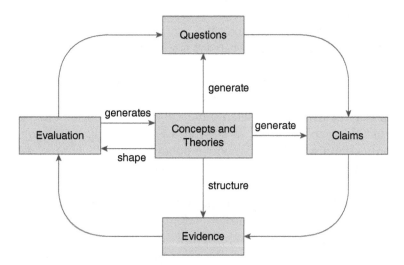

Figure 2.2 Concepts and theories shape, and are shaped by, the circuit of knowledge

Adapted from Sherratt et al., 2000, p. 18.

Some of the implications of these points are discussed further in sections 6.1, 6.2 and 8.2. For now, what you need to grasp is that essay writing in the social sciences is distinguished by its emphasis on the use of well-researched *evidence* to support arguments, and on *theory* as central to the process by which we build accounts of social worlds. Your own writing will need to engage with both.

Formal essays also have a number of distinctive stylistic elements that distinguish them from other forms of writing. Chapter 11 looks at some of the main differences – and similarities – between essays and other typical forms of social science written assessment, such as report writing or 'essay-style' exam answers.

2.3 Common errors in essays

Having identified what distinguishes a social science essay we can return to the more practical task of how to write one. This process is elaborated in the chapters that follow, but before getting into the details of this, we should think about what commonly goes wrong in essay writing.

Perhaps the most common mistakes in essay writing, all of which can have an impact on your marks, are:

- Failing to answer the question;
- Failing to write using your own words;
- Poor use of social scientific skills (such as handling theory and evidence);
- Poor structure;
- Poor grammar, punctuation and spelling;
- Failing to observe the word limit (where this is specified).

Failing to answer the question sounds easy enough to avoid, but you might be surprised how easy it is to write a good answer to the wrong question. Most obviously, there is always the risk of misreading the question (suggestions on how to avoid this can be found in section 4.1). However, it is frequently the case that questions will 'index' a wider debate and will want you to review and engage with this. Thus, you need to avoid the danger of understanding the question but failing to connect it to the debate and the body of literature to which the question refers (this point is discussed more fully in sections 5.3 and 8.1). Equally, particularly on more advanced undergraduate courses, you are likely to be asked to work from an increasing range of sources. The dangers here include failing to select the *most* relevant material and failing to organize the material you have selected in a way that best fits the question. Therefore, make sure that you take time to read the question properly to ensure that you understand what is being asked. Next, think carefully about whether there is a debate that 'lies behind' the question. Then be sure to identify the material that addresses the question most fully.

Writing in your own words is crucial because this is the best way in which you can come to understand a topic, and the only way of demonstrating this understanding to your tutor. How to avoid 'plagiarism' (or copying what some-one else has already written or said) is dealt with in detail in section 12.5. The important point to remember is that if you do plagiarize, your essay risks receiving a fail grade, and if you plagiarize repeatedly you risk further sanc-tions. You must therefore always put arguments in your own words *except* when you are quoting someone verbatim (in which case you must use the appropriate referencing conventions, discussed in Chapter 10). One positive side of what might seem like a draconian rule is that you will remember better what you have put in your own words. This ensures that you will have the fullest possible understanding of your course. If there is an end-of-course exam, such an understanding will be a real asset.

Social science essays also need to demonstrate an effective use of social scientific skills. Perhaps the most obvious of these skills is the ability to deploy theory and evidence in an appropriate manner (as you saw in the pre-vious section, this is what distinguishes social scientific essay writing). However, particularly as you move on to more advanced courses, you should also keep in mind the need to demonstrate such things as confidence in han-dling social scientific concepts and vocabulary; an awareness of major debates, approaches and figures in your field; the ability to evaluate compet-ing arguments; and an awareness of potential uncertainty, ambiguity and the limits of knowledge in your subject. These are important because they indicate your ability to work creatively with the tools of the social scientist's trade (these issues are addressed throughout the following chapters).

An effective structure is important and pragmatic because it helps the per-son who marks your essay to understand what is going on. By contrast, a list of unconnected ideas and examples is likely to confuse – and will certainly fail to impress. The simplest way to avoid this is to follow the kind of essay writing conventions briefly outlined above and discussed in later chapters of this guide. Chapter 8, on the main body of the essay, is particularly relevant here, but you will also need to keep in mind the importance of a well-written introduction (see Chapter 7) and conclusion (see Chapter 9) to an effectively structured argument.

The ability to spell, punctuate and use grammar correctly is, generally speaking, something you are expected to have mastered prior to embarking on a degree-level course. As sections 8.4 and 12.4 explain, this is really a matter of effective communication. While it is the content of your essay that will win you the most marks, you need to be able spell, punctuate and use grammar effectively in order to communicate what you have to say. Major problems in this area will inevitably hold down your marks, so if this is an issue in your work, it would be a good idea to seek further help.

Finally, observing the word limit is important – and, as you probably realize, more difficult than it sounds. Further advice on this matter is available in section 12.1, but the simplest advice is always to check whether there is a word limit and what this is, and then to be ruthless with yourself, focusing only on the material that is most pertinent to the question. If you find that you have written more words than allowed, you will need to check for irrelevant discussions, examples, or even wordy sentence construction. Too few words may indicate that you have omitted essential points or evidence, written in an inappropriate 'shorthand' style, or that you haven't provided the depth or breadth of discussion required.

In light of the above, we can identify four golden rules for effective social scientific essay writing.

2.4 Four golden rules for writing a social science essay

Rule 1: Answer the question that is asked.

Rule 2: Write your answer in your own words.

Rule 3: Think about the content of your essay, being sure to demonstrate good social scientific skills.

Rule 4: Think about the structure of your essay, being sure to demonstrate good writing skills, and observe any word limit.

Summary

- A basic social science essay has the following: a title, an introduction, a main section, a conclusion, and a list of references.
- Essays in the social sciences are distinguished by their emphasis on the use of evidence to evaluate arguments and the use of theory to build accounts of the social world as well as stylistic conventions.
- There is some debate in the social sciences on the relationship between theory and evidence.
- There are four golden rules of social science essay writing:

  1 Answer the question that is asked.
  2 Write your answer in your own words.

3 Think about the content of your essay, being sure to demonstrate good social scientific skills.

4 Think about the structure of your essay, being sure to demonstrate good writing skills and observe any word limit.

Self-test

1 What are the two most important characteristics of social science writing?

2 What are the components of the circuit of knowledge? How does the circuit help us understand social science essays?

3 What are the most common errors made in social science essays?

4 What are the four 'golden rules'?

Don't forget! Visit **https://study.sagepub.com/redmanandmaples5** for more tasks and resources related to this chapter.

3

Stages of Writing, from Preparation to Final Version

- Read the question and any essay guidance notes
- Use feedback
- Identify and organize the relevant material: drafting an essay plan
- First draft to final version
- Time management

Here are some reminders for those of you already experienced in essay planning, and some suggestions for anyone coming to social science essay writing for the first time. In short, there are seven stages to writing an essay:

1. Reading and understanding the question
2. Identifying the relevant material
3. Making an essay plan
4. Writing a first draft
5. Reviewing the first draft and writing a second draft
6. Double-checking the administrative requirements of the essay
7. Writing a final version.

In this chapter, we will take an overview of these stages. In addition, we look at some other aspects of planning that you will encounter before you put pen to paper. Thorough preparation and planning is the basis of any good piece of written work, and it really is worth putting some effort into this.

3.1 Read the question and any essay guidance notes

The best advice anyone can offer you when you embark on an essay is to *read the question*. As you will see in Chapter 4, you need to spend time 'unpacking' the question and being certain you understand both what the content, or main topics or issues, of the essay should be, and how you are expected to address this (as indicated by the 'command' or 'process' words and type of question). Here we will examine the importance of this seemingly simple practice, and of considering any guidance you've been given, either as part of the essay question, or in the form of feedback on a previous essay.

Essay question guidance

In many universities, in addition to the question itself, you will be given guidance on how to answer the question. This may take the form of formally written notes, or it might be verbal instructions from your tutor. In either case, be certain you are clear about this guidance as there may be suggestions about source material, or caveats about areas that are precluded. Introductory level courses may also include guidance about how to structure your essay which you should follow to the letter.

Let's look at an example:

> **Outline the role of risk in contemporary society and the idea that we live in a risk society. Your essay should aim to show the role of the social sciences in understanding risks and how people live with them.**
>
> In this assignment, you are asked to produce a descriptive essay that considers the role of risk in contemporary society, to consider Ulrich Beck's argument that we live in a 'risk society', and to provide relevant examples, illustrations or case studies in support of this. You will need to utilize different forms of evidence to help you examine Beck's ideas. On this module, we have considered, for instance: the everyday ways of dealing with risks; the notion that defining risks depends on the complex and contested production of knowledge; the ways in which people perceive and act in relation to knowledge about risks; the role of experts in making risks known to the lay public; and the ways in which people live with and respond to expert ideas about risk. Remember to reference your sources in the body of the essay and to provide a list of references at the end. Word count: 1,250.
>
> (Adapted from DD101 'Introducing the Social Sciences', 2009J, Assignment Booklet 2, The Open University.)

This example is taken from a Level I or freshman year module, and the guidance is fairly specific. The students are told that they are producing a descriptive essay that outlines 'risk' and Ulrich Beck's argument that we live in a 'risk society' in particular. The second part of the question asks them to consider the kind of social science evidence that might be drawn upon in arguing that we live in a risk society, and gives examples of how this has been addressed on the module. However, the guidance also tells students to find case studies and other illustrative material – but which case studies or other examples is left to the students to decide for themselves.

There is also an implicit suggested structure to the essay. Can you make it out? First, students are asked to outline the idea of risk, and describe what Ulrich Beck means by 'risk society' – demonstrating their understanding of his argument. Second, they are asked to look at various bits of illustrative material, case studies or social scientific evidence to demonstrate a) what Beck means, and b) how people 'live with' risk. Third, students are asked to think about what social science brings to an understanding of 'risk' and the 'risk society' – this could involve looking at the 'circuit of knowledge' (see section 2.2), and showing how social scientists approach both ideas and evidence.

Finally, the guidance includes a word count. Your module or university will have guidelines on how much latitude there is in keeping to the word count. In many social science departments, you will find you are expected to keep to the word count, give or take 5 or 10 per cent. So, a 1,000 word essay could be between 950 and 1,050 or between 900 and 1,100 words long and still meet the word count requirement.

3.2 Use feedback

If this is not your first essay you are at a distinct advantage, especially if you have had individual feedback on previous work. Preparing to write a second, third, fourth (etc.) essay should begin with considering your prior achievements and any and all feedback you've had so far. Take a look at the box below.

What to do when your essay comes back

Maggie Coats
Maggie Coats is an Associate Lecturer at The Open University. These are her suggestions for learning from your last essay.

If you're like most other people, when you get an essay back you'll check the grade first, read any general comments from your tutor, and quickly flip through the rest looking for any major embarrassments. You'll probably read it with more care only if the tutor has written something particularly complimentary or irritating. However, learning from previous pieces of writing is an important way of building on your writing skills.

- Take a quick look at the score and any general comments. Feel pleased, angry or despairing, depending on your grade/mood, then put the essay aside until you are ready to look at it with a more 'objective' eye.
- Give yourself 20 to 30 minutes to look over the essay in detail – more if it is a longer essay.
- Re-read any general comments and note the main points.
- Re-read the essay itself, including your tutor's in-text or margin comments, then mark your responses to these comments. Do you agree or disagree? Is there anything you don't understand?
- Next, re-read the general or overview comments your tutor has made at the end of your essay. Can you see what the tutor is saying?
- Having gained a little perspective on your writing, what do *you* think of it? Did you: answer the question; provide the most relevant examples; muster a clear argument?
- On a separate sheet of paper, or in your learning journal, write down one or two key points that will improve your performance when writing the next assignment.

(Adapted from Coats, M. (undated) Handout Material 2.)

If you have reflected on previous work in this manner, you will be in a better position to tackle the essay at hand.

What to do if you don't get feedback, or feedback is minimal

At some colleges or universities, it is common not to get much in the way of individual feedback on your work. In this case, you may need to be a bit more industrious in figuring out what to do to improve your next assignment. Sometimes tutors will offer generic feedback to the whole class – things that most people did well or poorly. If this is the case, read through your essay, look at your essay plan (see below), and try to see where your own work has followed the good practice identified by your tutor, and likewise where it hasn't met your tutor's expectations. You can also use this book as a 'check' on your work. Of course you won't be able to use it to identify your understanding of subject content, but you will be able to use it to help you check whether you have read the question and followed its 'commands' (section 4.2). Upcoming chapters will help you identify whether you have written a useful introduction, a coherent main body, a convincing conclusion, and an accurate list of references (Chapters 7–10).

As Maggie Coats suggests, try to be objective when looking over your work – the idea is to learn from your previous work, so that you can improve in your next essay.

3.3 Identify and organize the relevant material: drafting an essay plan

Once you have a clear idea of what the question is asking, and particular areas you need to concentrate on improving, your next task is to identify and organize the material you will be using in your essay. We will look at researching and note-taking for essay writing in more detail in Chapter 5, and Chapters 7–10 consider the essential components of an essay. Here we offer a quick overview of some of the main activities you will need to do:

- Read through any existing notes that you have, from lectures, seminars or texts; read or re-read the book chapters or journal articles specified for this particular essay; and review recommended or linked websites. Make notes about all relevant material.
- Keep careful and detailed notes of all sources for your reference list (see Chapters 5 and 10).

Having identified the relevant material, you will need to organize this into a shape that addresses the question. Here are some suggestions for tackling this task:

- 'Wordstorm' your ideas for the essay (that is, jot down a list of questions and issues prompted by the question, all the relevant examples you can think of, and any other related evidence). For many people, this is most productively done with pen and paper, but if you wordprocess your notes you might like to use wordstorming software, like Wordle (www.wordle.net). This kind of software can help you see graphically where you have lots of material or ideas, and where your notes are lacking. To see a Wordle of this chapter, see Figure 3.1.
- Re-check your notes and add left-out material (do another search).
- Then link and order connected ideas and points. One way to do this is to draw a 'mind-map' or diagram of points relevant to the question. Mindmapping is very good for making strong visual links between different parts of an argument. Most people find mindmapping easiest using pen and paper, but there are software packages that help with mindmapping notes, such as Mindomo, Mindmap, Freemind or Tufts University's VUE – Visual Understanding Environment. Figure 3.2 shows an example of a Mindmup mindmap used to prepare for writing 'Essay 1' which appears in Chapter 14.
- Write out points, examples, ideas and connected theories on separate sheets of paper, 'Post-its', or index cards. Group and re-group these until you've got them in a logical order. Section 8.1 offers ideas for creating a 'logical progression' in your argument.

Figure 3.1   A Wordle of this chapter

- Write out a list, using numbers and sub-numbers or bullet points. This is a 'linear' essay plan for the main body of the essay (you can worry about the introduction and conclusion later). Figure 3.3 shows an example of a linear essay plan for writing 'Essay 1' which appears in Chapter 14.
- Ideas may come to you at unexpected moments – for these keep a notebook handy and jot them down.

You will see from Figures 3.2 and 3.3 that there is a familiar 'shape' to the essay. There is always an introduction, a conclusion and a reference list, and the main body of the essay commonly focuses on three key points. One of the skills you will develop as you write is selectivity. It is important not to write 'everything' you know about a subject, but to pick out the most essential points. Sometimes the essay question itself will indicate the most important areas to cover, and sometimes this will be suggested in any guidance notes. Sometimes, however, you will need to decide this for yourself. There are a number of tricks to this. The first is to look at your mindmap or linear notes and decide which points your essay can do without – that is, which points will make little difference to an understanding of the topic. The second is to identify the most important point – the issue or idea on which all other points hinge. The third is to ask the 'so what?' question. Put simply, if another student were to ask you 'so what?' about a key point you have identified, would you be able to answer? If not, either this point is less important to the essay, or you need to do some more reading and consolidating of your thoughts.

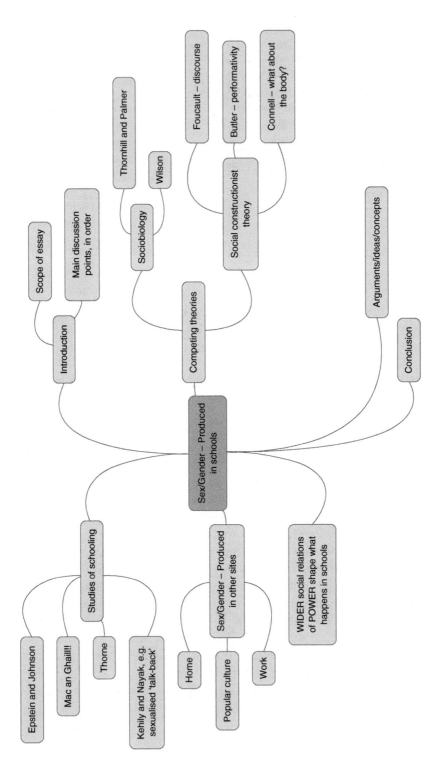

Figure 3.2 Example of a mindmap of 'Essay 1' in Chapter 14: 'School is a significant site in which sex/gender is produced'. Discuss.

'School is a significant site in which sex/gender is produced.' Discuss.

Introduction: main points, in order (write this last)

Main body

1. Social constructivism v. biological reductivism (Weedon, 1999; Foucault, 1977, 1984; Lacquer, 1990; Butler, 1993, 2004). 'Hard' and 'soft' social constructivism, e.g. issue of social agency (Butler, 1993 v. Connell, 1995).

2. The active production of sex/gender in schools: recent literature

   a. Thorne (1993) US elementary schools and teachers' talk
   b. Epstein and Johnson (1994) pupils' clothes
   c. Students as active agents, e.g. handball (Thorne, 1993), also mistletoe (Kehily and Nayak, 1996)
   d. Negotiating the curriculum and differentiated masculinities (Connell, 1993 and Mac an Ghaill, 1994)

3. Sex and gender and other subjectivities: masculinity/femininity and age, class, ethnicity, sexuality

   a. Epstein and Johnson (1998) 'intra-ethnic identification' (find quote about Shamira being a 'tart'?)
   b. Mac an Ghaill (1994) boys' sexualized talk
   c. Hmm – no room for age – class will be covered a bit with Mac an Ghaill
   d. Need to include POWER and wider social relations

Conclusion – review evidence, modification of social constructionist account, and note relation between sex/gender and other subject positions, restate claim.

Figure 3.3   An example of a linear essay plan of 'Essay 1' in Chapter 14

3.4 First draft to final version

We will look at the elements involved in structuring an essay in more detail in Chapters 7, 8 and 9, but here is an outline of the stages that follow on from formulating your essay plan, and that lead from first draft to final product:

- Write out the question at the beginning of your first draft so that you keep its exact wording in front of you to ensure you are answering the question that is asked.
- Working from your essay plan, begin writing a first draft. Do the best you can, but see it as a first draft and expect to make some improvements – you may need to revise your plan as the essay takes shape. Don't worry, this is perfectly normal!
- Once your first draft has some shape, you may need to go back to your notes to check your references, and you may also want to move sentences or even paragraphs around. Your second draft might deviate from your original plan – this is fine, as long as what you have written makes sense (proceeds in a logical fashion).
- If you have time, it is helpful to put the essay aside for at least a day to let the dust settle, show it to a friend or another student to get feedback, and then re-read the question and the essay yourself. Its strengths and weaknesses should now be a lot clearer to you.

- You are now in a position to write your definitive answer, and this is the time to consider more carefully your presentation (sentence structure, grammar, etc.), and to check for clarity of expression. It is good practice to 'spell check' your work, but remember the limits of spell check – you will still need to re-read your work to be sure it actually makes sense. Learn the difference between 'there', 'their' and 'they're', and where the possessive apostrophe goes, depending on whether a word is singular, plural or ends in an 's'.
- Ensure your reference list is complete and matches the actual citations you have made in the essay, and that you have followed the referencing style required by your course (see Chapter 10).
- Double-check any administrative requirements: is the essay double-spaced and in the right-sized font (some tutors specifically ask for a 12-point font so the essay is easier to read); have you inserted page numbers in the footer; is your name and/or student number, assignment number, etc., in the header?

Administrative requirements checklist:

- Is there a recommended format for the header – for instance, should you include your name or student number, the module title, tutor's name, date of submission, etc.?
- Are you expected to have a separate title page – what should be included?
- What is expected in the footer? Page numbers? Anything else?
- Is there a specified font or typeface, and should the essay be double-spaced? Is there a margin requirement?
- When and where is the assignment DUE? Is there a cut-off time, as well as a date? Is there a specific location, email or drop box?

When this is complete, submit the essay – and wait for feedback with quiet confidence.

3.5 Time management

As the previous sections in this chapter have begun to suggest, as you move from your initial preparation to writing your final draft, you will need to plan your time carefully. Effective time management involves being realistic. You will obviously want to set aside as much time as possible for your essay. However, other important commitments may mean that you need to structure the time available with care. As early as possible look in your diary and, working backwards from your submission date, identify when you are going to be able to do the work. Next, prioritize your tasks and allocate your time accordingly. For example, if you are clear about the question from the start, you will probably have to spend less time on research. If you spend adequate time planning your essay, you may well find that writing the first draft is much easier. As you move through your tasks, concentrate on achieving your major goals. For example, when (re-)reading for the essay, don't get distracted by material that is interesting but less relevant to the essay question. Similarly, when writing your first draft, try not to get bogged down crafting perfect sentences or clarifying a single point. Focus on putting the whole argument in place and then go back to re-work individual sections and improve your style. Good time management will not necessarily mean that producing an essay is free from stress, but it will allow you to make the most of your circumstances.

The following chapters of this guide offer more detailed help through the process of essay preparation and planning, and of first draft to final version – in short, putting together a social sciences essay.

Summary

- Make use of sources of guidance.
- Essay writing has seven principal stages:

  1 Reading and understanding the question
  2 Identifying the relevant material
  3 Making an essay plan
  4 Writing a first draft
  5 Reviewing the first draft and writing a second draft
  6 Double-checking the administrative requirements of the essay
  7 Writing a final version.

- Realistic time management is central to effective essay writing.

Self-test

1 What are the seven principal stages of writing an essay?
2 How can you use guidance notes – notes for the essay and notes on your previous work? How can these integrate with the guidance on offer in this book?
3 How do you prefer to organize your essay plan – with a mindmap? using linear notes? Have you tried out any planning software that might help you represent your thoughts?
4 How can you ensure you include the most important material in your essay plan?
5 How can you be sure you've met all the requirements of the assignment?
6 How can you ensure you will have enough time to complete your essay by the cut-off date?

Don't forget! Visit https://study.sagepub.com/redmanandmaples5 for more tasks and resources related to this chapter.

4

Matching the Answer to the Question

- Unpacking the question
- Command words and cognitive skills
- Types of social science essay questions

Social science questions are often composed of two parts: the topic, issue, idea or position you are expected to consider, and the actions or processes you are required to do. These processes require different cognitive skills at different levels – from the ability to describe to the ability to evaluate. In addition, many social science essay questions ask you to consider one or more critical positions or arguments that you are then required to advocate, compare and contrast, or evaluate, which at different levels of study can mean different things. 'Unpacking the question' can be a tricky business, but below we offer guidance on how to simplify the process and accurately match your answer to the question asked.

4.1 Unpacking the question

As noted in Chapter 2, perhaps the most common mistake students make is not answering the question that is set. In order to avoid this, a primary task is to read the question carefully and 'unpack' its instructions. As we showed in Chapter 3, this may include reading carefully any additional guidance and following that to the letter. In addition, however, you will need to unpack the question itself. In so doing you should:

- identify the 'content' words – these tell you what topics, issues and/or concepts you will be writing about;
- identify the 'command', or 'process' words (for example, 'discuss', 'evaluate', 'explore') – these tell you *how* you should answer the question: identifying the command words is just as important as identifying the content words, as we will demonstrate below.

Let's consider the question, *'The family in Britain is in crisis.' Discuss.*

'Family', 'Britain', and 'crisis' are the content words. So, the evidence, concepts, theories and claims that you need to explore should focus on whether there is a crisis in the family in Britain and what 'crisis' – and indeed 'family' – might mean in this context. There is an implicit claim here ('the family is in crisis') and an implicit counter-claim ('the family is not in crisis'). What then is the evidence? Evidence might include data on the percentage of children in foster care compared with ten or twenty or fifty years ago – which may lead you to consider changes to policy on social services interventions – or you could focus on the changing roles of men and women in the domestic and social spheres – and the evidence that this has had (or has not had) an impact on children's upbringing – or you may argue that the traditional notion of the family is something of a 'myth'... . Depending on the social science subject you are studying, the essay will have different emphases. Historical changes in family structures may be a focus of your course, so part of your evidence could include a comparison of family hierarchies in different eras, or your module may have emphasized an international approach, in which case some comparison with other nations might be relevant.

We will consider more examples of essay questions later, so you can get more of a feel for how the context of your subject will inflect your essays, but as you can see there are various possible ways to tackle the question's content. You will also need to remember that social scientists may dispute 'commonsense' definitions: some terms will have a specialist social science meaning which you may also need to 'unpack'.

'Discuss' is the command or process word: 'discuss' can allow for a wide interpretation of the approach to the essay content, but implies that at the very least you should explore evidence and theories for and against the statement (see below). 'Discuss' is a very common command, but there are other process words you will encounter frequently in social science essay questions: we explore some of these now.

4.2 Command words and cognitive skills

At university level, there is an expectation that you will demonstrate progression in terms of cognitive skills from your earlier to later written work. This expectation is broadly reflected in the types of command or process words used in essay questions. The box below provides a list and explanation of common command words, organized in terms of the general cognitive skills being tested.

Command or process words in essay questions

- **Description**

To describe something is to provide an account that tells the reader you know what something is and can depict its main features. Clear description is an important base-line social science skill and often follows observation. A fairly standard observation-description question might look something like this: 'With permission, observe the practice of a local amateur sports team. Describe what you have observed in terms of leadership, organization and participation'. In this case, the quality of description is dependent on your powers of observation. Description is not just about reporting observations, however. To describe a television show, you might indicate its genre, notable characters, 'stars', intended audience, audience figures, and also perhaps some aspects of the storyline, main topics or issues. For instance: '*Doctor Who* is a long-running science fiction television series produced by the British Broadcasting Corporation (BBC) that first aired in the UK in 1963. Considered idiosyncratically British and increasingly outdated, with parochial storylines, low-budget sets and clunky costumes, the original series ended in 1989. In 2005, however, the show relaunched: screenwriter Russell T. Davies drafted a new series and dramatic actor Christopher Eccleston took on the lead role. *Doctor Who* has since experienced a resurgence of popularity in the UK. It has also gained a larger international fan base, with BBC Worldwide exporting *Doctor Who* to over 50 countries'.

Table 4.1 'Description' process words

Describe	Give an (detailed) account of ...
Define	State the exact meaning of a word or phrase. In some cases it may be necessary or desirable to present different possible definitions, keeping in mind that 'commonsense' terms may be under dispute.
Depict	Show.
Identify	Find and describe an example or issue.
Illustrate	Make clear and explicit: this usually requires the use of carefully chosen examples.
State	Present in a brief, clear way.
What is/are ... ?	Identify and describe.

- **Summary**

Writing an effective summary demonstrates knowledge of information and/or ideas. The skill here is to distil information or ideas, often into a very few words. You may find that summary-type questions will benefit from graphics or tables as part of your answer. To summarize a journal article, you would give the name of the author, date and title of the publication, indicate the article's key points, the main examples offered, and the author's conclusion. At a more advanced level, you might situate the article in its academic subject context, indicating if it is responding to or part of a particular debate or tradition of thought. It is also common to be asked to summarize the content of, for instance, a policy document as part of a wider essay question. Being able to summarize is a key skill for writing a précis or an abstract; it is also essential for indicating a setting, such as a school or hospital, without getting bogged down in detail whilst indicating to your tutor your understanding of a location's most significant features and context.

Table 4.2 'Summary' process words

Outline	Give the main features or general principles of a subject, omitting minor details and emphasizing structure and arrangement.
Summarize	Give a concise, clear account of a topic or argument, presenting the chief factors and omitting minor details and examples.
What are the main features of … ?	Select the more significant features (of an issue, project, etc.) and present them coherently.

- **Interpretation**

Interpretation moves you beyond description to demonstrating understanding – for instance, by suggesting connections between features. For example: 'Compare Bauman's and Veblen's perspectives on consumption'. This question suggests that there are (at least) two competing theories that can help to explain consumption. At a basic level, there is some description and summary necessary to answer this question: you would need to summarize both Bauman's and Veblen's theories in order to compare them. However, there is also some interpretation or 'sensemaking' required. Particularly at a higher level, you would need to consider how it is that Veblen and Bauman arrive at different positions – what are the social contexts of their writing? This might include some mention of the different time periods in which they were writing (Veblen – late 1800s; Bauman – late 1900s), and other social contexts.

(Continued)

(Continued)

Table 4.3   'Interpretation' process words

Compare	Look for similarities and differences between, and – at more advanced levels – reach conclusions about which is preferable and justify this clearly (see *Evaluation*).
Compare and contrast	Find some points of common ground between x and y and show where or how they differ.
Contrast	Set x and y in opposition in order to bring out the differences sharply.
Distinguish or differentiate between …	Show the differences between x and y (and maybe z).

- **Discussion**

As in ordinary life, a discussion involves recognizing two or more positions in relation to a topic or question, how they differ from each other, and how valid or effective an account each offers. A public debate, with proposers and seconders, is one kind of discussion, but others may be less formally structured. Discussions may be at different levels – from more descriptive accounts of different positions, through to critical, evaluative accounts that identify the value basis and strengths and weaknesses of different positions. Unlike an ordinary, coffee-shop-type discussion, academic discussion should develop an argument in a logical and coherent fashion and reach a conclusion. 'Discuss' questions may be the most common questions you will come across in social science. The word 'discuss' often follows a provocative or contentious statement, for instance: '"Strong leadership at the senior level drives National Health Service efficiency." Discuss'. In this case, there is a claim offered in the question's quotation – it is up to you to discuss the merits or otherwise of that claim by looking at the evidence and the logic of the claim, and any attendant argument (or theories on which the claim is based). Note that you are not asked definitively to agree or disagree: you may find convincing points on both sides of the debate, or you might – at the higher levels of study in particular – take issue with the basis of the question, perhaps by interrogating what is meant by 'leadership' or 'efficiency'.

Table 4.4   'Discussion' process words

Consider	Look at two (or more) sides of an argument, and present the logic, evidence, etc., of both sides.
Debate	Set up a claim or argument, presenting evidence for and against.

Discuss	Present two (or more) sides of an issue or argument and any implications.
What arguments can be made for and against the view that … ?	Look at both sides of an argument.

- **Explanation**

This deepens understanding by identifying causes. Often 'explain'-type questions are attached to historical shifts or changes. 'Explain' questions can also be used to set up an exploration of issues around difference. For instance: 'Account for the difference in wages between men and women in the USA, before and after the Equal Pay Act (1963)'. The task here is two-fold: to discuss that there are differences in wages, and then to explain the socio-historical contexts that led to pay disparity and the different socio-historical (and employment) contexts that maintain (a lesser) disparity. At the higher levels, you might raise related questions, such as other socio-demographic variables that lead to differences in pay (age, race, ethnicity, etc.). You may have noticed that we have avoided using the term 'cause': the social, political and economic relations that lead to differences (in pay, for example) are rarely the result of a single cause. 'Explanation' allows you to show a deeper understanding of correlations and the complexities surrounding these.

Table 4.5   'Explanation' process words

Account for	Explain, clarify, give reasons for….
Explain	Give details about how and why it is so.
How/Why is it … ?	Give an explanation, including the reasons for….

- **Evaluation**

This requires understanding that is genuinely critical and involves either testing the strengths and weaknesses of an explanation or considering the degree of success of an action, policy or argument. The former can be achieved by comparing the explanation to particular cases or examples and asking whether the argument can in fact be backed up by evidence. In the latter case, evaluation asks you to judge the effectiveness of a policy or action by looking for cases where the action has been worthwhile or successful and also for cases where things have not worked out – and to provide a balanced, but critical, analysis of this. Similar skills are involved in both instances: you are effectively making an argument on the pros and cons of a particular view or approach – weighing them up, in light of the coherence of the

(Continued)

(Continued)

argument, or the strength of the evidence. A more 'evaluative' version of the equal pay question above might look something like this: 'Evaluate the claim that the Equal Pay Act of 1963 has made little or no difference to the wages of women in the workplace'. Here the task is to evaluate the claim that the Equal Pay Act was useless. This rendering of the question will require (at least) two lines of enquiry: that on the one hand there have been other reasons why women's pay has improved, and on the other that – despite legislation – unequal pay remains a significant issue. In order to explore these, you would need to find evidence, probably at least partly in the form of statistics, to demonstrate both change and stasis, and theories that explain why federal legislation has been helpful/unhelpful in promoting social and economic change.

Table 4.6   'Evaluation' process words

Assess	Determine the value of, weigh up.
Criticize/Critically assess	Make a judgement (backed by a discussion of the evidence and/or reasoning involved) about the merit of theories or opinions or about the facts of a matter.
Evaluate	Make an appraisal of the worth/validity/effectiveness of something in light of its accuracy or usefulness.
How far … /To what extent … ?	Usually involves looking at evidence/arguments – for and against – and weighing them up.
Justify	Show adequate grounds for decisions or conclusions, answer the main objections likely to be made about them.

- **Other common process words**

Table 4.7   Other common process words

Analyse	Resolve into its component parts. Examine critically or minutely. 'Analyse' may be used as a descriptive command word at the higher levels of study, or it might be used to indicate an 'evaluate' requirement.
Examine the …	Look in detail at this line of argument.

> You may also find that many questions are composites: '**Evaluate** the claim that … . **Illustrate** your answer with … .'; '**Give an example of** … . **Explain**, drawing on Marx or Weber, how … .'
>
> Composites mean that you are required to demonstrate more than one skill: you will need to determine which skill carries more 'weight' and adjust your answer accordingly.

(Adapted from Sue Cole, Associate Lecturer, and Pauline Harris, Assistant Staff Tutor (undated), 'Handout Material 2', and Phil Sarre, Senior Lecturer in Geography (2009), 'Environment: Project and Assignment Booklet, 2010', and from The Open University's Student Home Study Skills website (internal access only).)

Although there is not a strict progression of cognitive skills in the social sciences, you will probably find that you are asked for more description (knowledge) in the early stages of your studies and more evaluation (understanding) in the later stages. Also, as you progress, it will be expected that the descriptions you *are* asked to produce will be more detailed, complex or subtle. Evaluations may involve more variables, or more difficult issues. In broad terms, you will be demonstrating greater knowledge and increasingly complex understanding in your intermediate and advanced essays.

4.3 Types of social science essay questions

Broadly speaking, there are three 'types' of questions in the social sciences: advocacy, compare and contrast, and evaluation questions. Each type of question suggests a particular format, or structure, for your essay. At the earlier and later stages of your studies these different types of questions will require different skills and, therefore, different sorts of answers.

Advocacy questions

Advocacy questions ask you to outline or explain and illustrate a single issue, topic or argument. You might think of advocacy answers as 'making a case' for a particular idea. Examples of this kind of question would include the following:

- How have changes to the way in which the production of food is organized affected both the UK and other parts of the world? Illustrate your answer with relevant examples.
- What is the role of the judiciary in the law-making process? Include a discussion of statutory interpretation and the system of precedent.

- What are the basic assumptions about humanistic psychology? How are these reflected in methods for encouraging growth?
- 'Improvements in learning in the classroom appear to have little to do with mass testing of children.' Explain.

Advocacy answers

A basic answer to an advocacy question might look something like this:

Introduction

- Indicate the broad content of your essay.
- Indicate what you see as the core issue(s) and how you intend to approach this (these) – in other words, say what you will be 'advocating' or speaking about.

Main section

- Provide a brief overview of the issue, topic or argument. Depending on the length of the essay, you may have space to include some contextualization of the issue as well.
- Provide a more detailed breakdown of the key components of the issue, topic or argument – in other words, develop your 'case'.
- Give examples to illustrate these points.
- Briefly explore weaknesses in the viewpoint that you've been asked to advocate and indicate alternative ways of thinking about the issues.

Or, as another example, you may decide to do the following:

- Provide a brief overview of the issue, topic or argument.
- Then, in more detail, make your 'case': outline one component of the issue, topic or argument and illustrate with a relevant example; outline the second component of the issue, topic or argument and illustrate with another example; outline the third component, etc.
- Briefly explore weaknesses in the approach and indicate alternative ways of addressing the issues.

The nature of the question and the material you have chosen to use will dictate the structure of an advocacy answer. However, it will generally be expected that you will build a 'case' in a logical and convincing manner.

Conclusion

- Recap key points and illustrations. Give a final assessment of the usefulness of the approach.

Remember, this is only a basic format covering the major ingredients of an advocacy question and you shouldn't follow it slavishly.

Advocacy questions in relation to 'introductory', 'intermediate' and 'advanced' essay writing

Advocating a position is one of the more basic undergraduate essay-writing skills. As you develop 'intermediate' and 'advanced' skills, you will be expected to show an increasing ability to outline and illustrate more complex positions, a greater understanding of their potential weaknesses, and an increased awareness of alternative ways of addressing the issues.

Compare and contrast questions

Compare and contrast questions ask you to: outline points of common ground between competing positions; explore ways in which they differ, identifying how different positions often appeal to different kinds of evidence; and, sometimes, compare the particular positions to other positions in the same field. Examples of this kind of question would include:

- Compare and contrast two different explanations of 'racial' divisions.
- Contrast the argument that 21st century globalization is mainly about the production of flows, with the argument that prioritizes territories.
- Compare and contrast Lacanian and 'British School' psychoanalytic accounts of identity formation.

Compare and contrast answers

A basic answer to a compare and contrast question might look something like this:

Introduction

- Indicate the broad content of the essay.
- Outline the comparisons you intend to make – the key areas of common ground and the differences between the issues/positions, etc.

Main section

- Outline position (a) and position (b).
- Identify key points of common ground between these positions and compare them.

- Identify supplementary points of common ground between these positions and compare them.
- Identify and explore key points of contrast between position (a) and position (b).
- Identify and explore supplementary points of contrast between position (a) and position (b).
- If necessary, identify and explore significant ways in which position (a) and position (b) can be contrasted to a third competing position (c).
- Briefly evaluate the merits of these positions.

Once again, you will almost certainly need to adapt this basic format to fit different questions and different material. For instance:

- There may be an obvious debate 'behind' the question that requires you to emphasize the ways in which two contrasting positions *share* a common orientation that is in competition with a third position. This might be the case in the third of the example questions. It reads: 'Compare and contrast Lacanian and "British School" psychoanalytic accounts of identity formation'. Here you might need to emphasize that competing psychoanalytic approaches share a common belief in the importance of unconscious processes, a belief not shared by, for example, ethnomethodological, Foucauldian and some other social constructionist accounts. A debate of this kind may require you to scale down the extent to which you compare and contrast positions (a) and (b) in order for you to contrast these to a third position (c).
- Equally, you may decide to compare a key point from positions (a) and (b) and then move straight on to contrast a key point from each position. You would then compare another point and contrast another point, and so on. This would be an alternative to exploring all the points of comparison in one section, and then all the points of contrast in another. Ask yourself which method works best in relation to the question set and the material with which you are working.

The trick is to adapt this basic structure to a shape that best fits your requirements.

Conclusion

- Summarize the major points of comparison and contrast between the positions and briefly recap which is most persuasive and why.

Compare and contrast questions in relation to 'introductory', 'intermediate' and 'advanced' essay writing

There is likely to be an increased expectation that you will be able to compare and contrast positions and arguments as you move beyond your introductory studies. In developing 'intermediate' and 'advanced' skills you will be expected to show an increasing ability to compare and contrast more complex positions, emphasize key points, relate the positions under analysis to relevant alternative positions in the same field, and write from 'within' one or another position – which means adopting the conceptual world-view and language of a perspective or theory (see section 8.2). You will also be expected to show greater sophistication in your analysis, and greater confidence in showing a reasoned preference for one position over another.

Evaluation questions

As noted above, evaluation questions ask you to examine arguments for and against a particular position or issue and to assess their relative strengths and weaknesses. Examples of this kind of question would include:

- To what extent does citizenship depend on having a modern welfare state?
- 'Conceptual categories are clearly defined and tightly structured as hierarchically organized mental representations.' To what extent do you agree with this view?
- Critically evaluate the definition of work as 'paid employment'.
- Select a healthcare policy that relates to your own area of nursing practice. Discuss the origins of the policy, its authorship, and how it has been developed. Critically examine the context of the policy and to what and to whom the policy relates, and identify its potential to impact positively on patient and client care.

Evaluation answers

A basic answer to an evaluation question might look something like this:

Introduction

- Indicate the broad content of the essay.
- Briefly express the considerations that will go into your evaluation.

Main section

- Outline the position(s) or issue(s).
- Give arguments (that is, chains of logical reasoning) and evidence in support of the position.
- Give arguments, supported by evidence, that go against, question or show limitations to the position.
- Weigh up the arguments for and against the position.

In light of different material and different questions you may well want to adapt this basic format. For instance:

- You could start with the 'weaker' of the arguments in the main section and follow it up with 'stronger' arguments. Will this convince the reader of your point of view more effectively?
- Rather than exploring the first position (a) and then the second and competing position (b), you could explore one point from position (a) and contrast it with a parallel point from position (b), then explore another point from position (a) and contrast it with another point from position (b), and so on. Does this clarify or confuse your overall argument?

As with answers to advocacy or compare and contrast questions, you will need to decide how best to structure the argument in light of the question asked and the material used to answer it. Equally, you will need to emphasize different sections (the exploration of arguments for and against, the evaluation section) depending on the nature of the question.

As before, the trick is to adapt this basic structure to a shape that best fits your requirements.

Conclusion

- Summarize, making an explicit statement as to which position (if any) you find most convincing (given the evidence and logic of the argument), and to what extent or with what caveats.

Evaluation questions in relation to 'introductory', 'intermediate' and 'advanced' essay writing

As a skill, evaluation is undoubtedly more challenging than advocacy. Consequently, in developing 'intermediate' and 'advanced' skills, you will be expected to show an increasing ability to evaluate more complex or nuanced positions, increased awareness of alternative ways of addressing the issues, and more confidence in showing a reasoned preference for one position over another. Additionally, although not in all circumstances, you will be expected to demonstrate your ability to write from 'within' a perspective or theory, including evaluating evidence and arguments through the 'lens' of this worldview (see section 8.2).

Summary

- Make sure you have read the question, which involves 'unpacking' its component parts.
- Social science questions frequently have two main components: 'content' words, and 'command' or 'process' words.

- Content words relate to the subject matter at hand and may need defining. Remember that social scientists often take issue with 'commonsense' definitions.
- Command words reflect the various cognitive skills being tested in a given essay.
- Advocacy questions ask you to outline and illustrate a particular issue, topic or argument.
- Compare and contrast questions ask you to identify and explore points of comparison and contrast between competing positions.
- Evaluation questions ask you to explore arguments for and against competing positions and to evaluate their relative strengths and weaknesses.
- Suggested structures should be adapted in light of the question and the material under discussion.
- As you develop 'intermediate' and 'advanced' skills you will be expected to show greater confidence and ability in deploying essay structuring skills. Your essays will also need to demonstrate more nuanced, complex and comprehensive understanding in terms of process (following the commands) and content (exploring the subject matter).

Self-test

1 What is the most common reason for a well-written essay to receive a low mark?
2 What is a 'content' word?
3 What is a 'process' or 'command' word?
4 As you move into intermediate- and advanced-level studies, what sorts of cognitive skills will your essays increasingly test?
5 What is: an 'advocacy' question; a 'compare and contrast' question; an 'evaluation' question?
6 What are the similarities and differences between the suggested basic structures of advocacy, compare and contrast, and evaluation questions?

Don't forget! Visit **https://study.sagepub.com/redmanandmaples5** for more tasks and resources related to this chapter.

5

Reading, Note-taking and Literature Searches

- Reading
- Taking notes
- Academic literature searches and gathering data

Before you begin writing your essay, or even planning to write your essay, you will have done quite a lot of preparation. This chapter outlines what that preparation will entail, but it cannot describe in detail all of the activities students undertake as part of their studies – for that, you may wish to look at other books that cover, for instance, university-level study skills, or literature searches. Instead, we look at the work that is core to preparing for essay writing.

5.1 Reading

Without a doubt the most crucial skill that you will need to deploy in preparing to write an essay is reading, closely followed by note-taking. Strong writers are generally effective and often avid readers. Reading academic material has a number of purposes – such as preparing for a seminar, gaining a general familiarity with a new subject, or filling in 'gaps' in your knowledge related to a specific lecture or seminar. However, here we are going to focus on a very instrumental approach to reading: purposeful reading to prepare for essay writing.

There are two main sorts of purposeful reading for essay writing – the first is 'skim' reading, the second is deeper or 'close' reading.

Skim reading

Skim reading involves looking at a book, article, chapter or website at a glance. The idea is to get a quick sense of whether the source is going to be useful for your purposes.

With a recommended textbook, you can begin by looking up a key word in the contents pages and finding the relevant chapter. Remember you are trying to find out information that will help you with your essay, so:

- keep your essay title on a piece of paper in front of you while you are reading.

Here is an example from a social sciences course on Environment:

Essay question: *According to the 1992 GATT (General Agreement on Tariffs and Trade) report, trade and environment are 'mutually supportive'. To what extent does the global trade in Colombian roses support this claim?*

The required textbook for the module includes a chapter entitled, 'Trading with the environment', by Annie Taylor (2003).

- Read the introductory paragraph.

One wet morning in December 1999, a crowd of about 50,000 people gathered on the streets of downtown Seattle. It was to become a historic protest, the first of many similar large-scale demonstrations. There were representatives from a huge range of groups: US steelworkers, consumer groups, development groups such as Oxfam, environmentalists such as the Royal Society for the Protection of Birds and Friends of the Earth, and animal rights groups. And it was not just organized groups – there were also individuals with no organized base. The real importance of the protest lies in the fact that so many people came together with a shared and unshakeable belief that the cause of the problems on which they were campaigning related to economic globalization and more particularly to the management of global trade. They chose Seattle on the first three days of December 1999 ... because that is where the World Trade Organization (WTO) was holding its Annual Ministerial Meeting.

(Taylor, A. (2003) 'Trading with the environment', in Bingham, N., Blowers, A. and Belshaw, C. (eds), *Contested Environments*, Milton Keynes/Chichester, OU/Wiley, p. 172.)

On the surface of it, there is little here that relates directly to the essay question, though there is something about global trade that sounds promising and a mention of environmentalists. In short, on the basis of the introduction to this chapter, we can't be sure it will be helpful.

- The next stage is to look up the question's content words in the book's index, or if the source is online to conduct a key word search.

There are a number of content words in this essay question: GATT, (global) trade, environment and Colombian roses. If we look in the book's index for 'GATT' there are five citations, including two specifically on the Report on Trade and the Environment. 'Global trade' has lots of citations, but three that are on roses. 'Environment' also has lots of citations, including two on environment and global trade. 'Roses' has three citations linked with global trade, as well as a number of other citations. This chapter looks now to be quite useful, despite the unpromising introduction.

- You might now decide to 'skim read' the chapter, noting particularly helpful sections.

There are different techniques for skim reading: reading the first and last paragraphs in a chapter, then the first and last lines in each 'promising' section, as identified by your index search; scanning through the whole piece, looking out for key authors, words or phrases and reading the paragraphs nearest these; reading only the paragraphs or pages indicated from your index search.

Skim reading is particularly useful if you are still not certain that the text will help you with your essay. Skim reading can also be an efficient way of finding pithy quotes, or examples to support your argument. Where you find particularly helpful sections, remember to note precisely where they are (the page numbers), and how you think they might help you when you come to write your essay (see section 5.2).

Using the tactic above, I found a short paragraph on the effects of rose production on the environment that could support the *counter-argument* that global trade is *not* supportive of the environment:

Forests are cleared to make room for the farms. Once the farms are operating the flowers need lots of water to make them grow and the rose farms draw heavily from local water supplies. Around the town of Madrid in Colombia the water level in the aquifer has fallen from 20 metres to 200 metres, and water now has to come from Bogotá. The pesticides and fertilizers, if not properly treated, run off to pollute local rivers. Because local farmers use the river water for their agriculture, the local produce that they live off – vegetables, grains and grazing pasture livestock – are also affected. (Taylor, 2003, p. 14)

Again scanning, I saw a neat phrase that could be used in a sentence that supports a balanced approach to trade and environment. Taylor says that 'trade is not an unquestionable villain' (2003, p. 176). I like the sound of this phrase, and if I decide that the evidence supports the balanced view, I think I would be hard pressed to find a pithier way to express this.

Close reading

Once you have decided that the chapter (or article, or webpage) is going to be useful, you will want to read most or all of it, with purpose and with an analytical or critical approach (see section 6.1). In part, this means being an active reader – 'interrogating' the text and being 'physical' with it, asking critical questions as you read and taking notes (see section 5.2) that will be useful for your essay. Active reading is a skill that you can develop, and is essential to good social science practice.

- Read critically and with purpose.

Tom Burns and Sandra Sinfield, who are specialist lecturers in learning development at London Metropolitan University, suggest some generic questions you should ask yourself as you begin reading in more depth. These are shown in Table 5.1 to help you organize your thoughts.

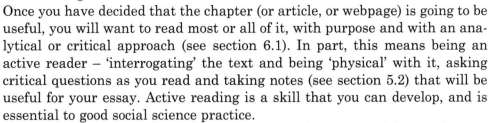

Essay question: *According to the 1992 GATT (General Agreement on Tariffs and Trade) report, trade and environment are 'mutually supportive'. To what extent does the global trade in Colombian roses support this claim?*

Table 5.1

Essay topic: *For this bit of reading, I am going to focus on the claim that:* 'the production of roses for global trade is mutually supportive of the environment'.	*Author/title of article/contents (Reference)* Taylor, A. (2003) 'Trading with the environment', in Bingham, N., Blowers, A. and Belshaw, C. (eds), *Contested Environments,* Milton Keynes/Chichester, OU/Wiley.
Why am I reading this?	I need to know more about why rose production for global trade might be environmentally harmful/helpful/neutral.
What am I looking for?	*Evidence that the production of roses is:* 1 Supportive of the environment 2 Environmentally neutral (or there are benefits of trade that outweigh the harm) 3 Not supportive of the environment

(Continued)

(Continued)

	Arguments: 1 Pros and cons of the global trade in roses (more theoretical) 2 Names of authors and theorists who have written on this subject *Supplementary material:* 1 Pithy quotes that can enliven my writing
How will I store the information?	I can make notes in the margin of the book (if I own it), in my notebook, or in my online notepad, following the key areas outlined in 'what am I looking for?': I can mark up the text with 'evidence: rose production/trade harmful to environment', or 'argument: free trade helps development', etc.
Where will I use the information?	The short answer is 'in my essay', but see below for a more detailed approach to this.
Which bit of my assignment will it help me with?	This will depend on how I structure my essay, but I think it will be useful for a lot of the main points. To get started, I think I will organize the essay into three main parts: 1 Arguments that global trade is damaging to the environment, with specific evidence from the trade in and production of roses. 2 Arguments that global trade can bring benefits to the environment or other benefits that outweigh the harm to the environment, with specific evidence from the trade in and production of roses. 3 A discussion that weighs up the evidence for and against, in light of an analysis of the different vested interests in a) continuing global trade and b) environmental conservation.
How will I know when I have what I need?	This is the tricky bit, particularly for social scientists, who tend to find more questions the more they read. However, there are two pragmatic answers: 1 When I can meet the requirements of this section of the assignment, according to whether I have addressed the different elements of the circuit of knowledge. So I need to ask: whether I have gathered strong (well-supported) evidence, and counter-evidence; can I explain the arguments or claims of the different proponents; can I explain the concepts used to develop this topic? 2 When I have run out of time. (This highly pragmatic approach may surprise you, but it is a reality of essay writing that you will have a deadline to meet.)

(Adapted from: Burns, T. and Sinfield, S. (2008) *Essential Study Skills*, London/Thousand Oaks, Sage, p. 159.)

Once you have your reading objectives in mind, you can start to read analytically and critically. This kind of active reading ensures that you remain engaged with the text and will help you remember what you have read. As you read, ask yourself the following questions.

Overview:

- What is the main idea here? The main topic of a paragraph is usually revealed in the first sentence (sometimes called the 'topic sentence'). Highlight (or note down) the main (topic), word (or phrase).

Argument(s):

- What is the author's argument?
- Where is the author coming from? Are they e.g. Marxist or neo-conservative? Are they e.g. free-market liberals or radical environmentalists? Do they have a feminist perspective?
- Have I encountered this argument before? Where? Make a note of who else would support this view.
- Have I come across a counter-argument? Where? (Again, make connections, jot them down.)

Evidence:

- What evidence is being offered?
- Is the evidence valid? Why do I think it is or is not valid?
- How does this change what I have already read/heard? (Cross-referencing in this way is very active reading.)

Summary thoughts/notes:

- What is the author's final point? (Usually the 'point' is in the final sentence of a paragraph. Notice what the author intended the paragraph to do.)
- What do I think?

(Adapted from: Burns, T. and Sinfield, S. (2008) *Essential Study Skills*, London/Thousand Oaks, Sage, pp. 160–1.)

Read the following excerpt from Kate Nash's (2009) article on citizenship and human rights.

Super-citizens

Within the legal status of 'full citizenship' there is a marked difference between what we might call 'super-citizens' and 'marginal citizens' in relation to human rights.

(Continued)

(Continued)

Super-citizens have all the rights of citizens but increasingly, in a globalizing, deregulated political economy, citizenship does not tie them to states because they own the means of production or are in possession of secure employment or marketable skills that enable mobility across borders. Super-citizens are those Craig Calhoun calls 'frequent flier' elite cosmopolitans (Calhoun, 2003).

This group has very little material interest as a group in human rights except insofar as human rights policies may succeed in making the world generally more stable and profitable. Their protected mobility comes from their citizenship status as well as from their wealth and/or skills. When faced with unstable or dangerous political conditions, super-citizens are more likely to fly home or to appeal to the authorities of the states to which they belong to intervene on their behalf than they are to claim human rights. On the other hand, they may be more likely to identify with cosmopolitanism and human rights than other people. Super-citizens may be involved in the extension of human rights as professionals – especially as lawyers, leaders of International Non-Governmental Organizations, or researchers – though they would not generally expect to see themselves as the subjects of human rights claims. With a cool detachment from de-moded nationalist fervour, they may also be more likely than others to celebrate specifically cosmopolitan virtues, including the adherence to principles of individual human rights (Turner, 2002).

(Nash, K. (2009) 'Between citizenship and human rights', *Sociology*, vol. 43, no. 6, Dec., pp. 1067–83, p. 1073.)

Here is our summary of the excerpt, using Burns' and Sinfield's prompts:

- The first sentence suggests that 'human rights' are unevenly available, depending on whether one is a 'super-citizen' or 'marginal citizen'.
- Super-citizens have global mobility due to employment skills or other status, and due to financial security may not see themselves as needing 'human rights' protection.
- From this section the author's 'take' or 'position' is not clear, but Nash may be arguing against a simplistic understanding of 'cosmopolitanism'. There is an area of globalization research that looks at cosmopolitanism as a noticeable feature of contemporary political and cultural engagement.
- She cites Turner and Calhoun, but does she agree with Calhoun?
- There is no direct evidence for her claims, but Nash cites Turner regarding the ways super-citizens might see themselves in relation to cosmopolitanism and human rights. (N.B. May need to *look up Turner*.)
- The final sentence argues that super-citizens embrace cosmopolitanism and believe in individual human rights.

You may have noticed other key ideas, or summarized this section somewhat differently; perhaps your field is in human rights or globalization and you bring with you background understandings that inflect your reading. The point here is to think about *how* you read, and to help yourself read actively. Having read the rest of the article, or found out more about what Calhoun or Turner have to say, the thoughts above may well be revised – reading actively, however, enables this.

5.2 Taking notes

You will have gathered from the previous section that taking notes is integral to active reading. Note-taking is quite a personal thing, but there is good evidence to suggest that the more active you are in taking notes in your own words, the more you will recall. Generally speaking, you should write questions, comments and translations of material in your own words as much as possible. How you form your notes, however, will depend on a number of factors. As our purpose in this book is to prepare you for essay writing, we will focus on those note-taking techniques most productive for short-term memory and making useful materials accessible for writing:

- Notes for essays should be selective. In other words, you should try to focus on the material that is most relevant for your assignment, ignoring more peripheral material, however interesting it may be.
- Notes should be short. There is no point in rewriting the whole of a chapter. You are better off writing a summary, with a clear citation so you can go back to the original text if you need to.
- With the exception of direct quotations (which should be short and used sparingly), notes should be in your own words as this helps retention and is an important stage in essay writing.
- Notes should be well-organized and clearly written so that you can refer back to them easily.

Margin notes

Hopefully, you will already be familiar with marking up your textbooks with a variety of notes in the margins – comments, questions, connections with other authors, etc. (Please remember, though, if you don't own the text, don't write on it.) Or you might use track-changes to add 'margin' notes to downloaded documents. This is good reading and note-taking practice. When it comes to writing your essays, however, margin notes are not very accessible.

Note-taking in notebooks or on index cards

Because margin notes are great at helping retention, but less good for helping you organize an example or argument in preparation for essay writing, you will need to develop additional note-taking strategies. Some students prefer to adopt a 'linear' or 'outline' style – lists with headings and sub-headings. This is a helpful technique for summarizing chapters, articles, lectures, etc., and short summaries are easy to refer to when you come to do your writing.

A short TED talk (www.ted.com) by Celeste Headlee (2016) on '10 ways to have a better conversation' (www.ted.com/talks/celeste_headlee_10_ways_to_have_a_better_conversation) might be summarized as shown in the box below.

Headlee cites studies that suggest social and political polarization is acute, and argues that this has something to do with diminishing conversation skills. As a radio host, Headlee spends her time interviewing people. She says the conversation skills of talking and listening that she uses professionally are the same as she uses in her everyday life. She has 10 rules for better conversations:

1 'Don't multi-task', be 'in' the conversation completely.
2 'Don't pontificate', instead be open to the other person's ideas. Nice Bill Nye quote: 'Everyone you will ever meet knows something that you don't'.
3 Ask open-ended, not closed, questions.
4 Pay attention to the speaker, rather than thinking about the point *you* were hoping to make.
5 If you don't know something, don't pretend you do.
6 'It's not about you': don't take the speaker's experience away from them by equating it with your experience.
7 Try not to repeat yourself.
8 Avoid pernickety details.
9 Most importantly, listen. Nice Calvin Coolidge quote: 'No man ever listened himself out of a job'. If you aren't listening, then it isn't a conversation.
10 'Be brief'.

Final summary: Headlee says 'be interested in other people', and always 'be prepared to be amazed'. If you are engaged in this way, you will enjoy better conversations.

Other students prefer to take 'mindmap' notes (see, for example, Figure 5.1).

Index cards are a note-taking option preferred by many students as they encourage 'thinking in shorthand'. Like any other paper-based notes, index cards can include lists, mindmaps, definitions, case studies, summaries of

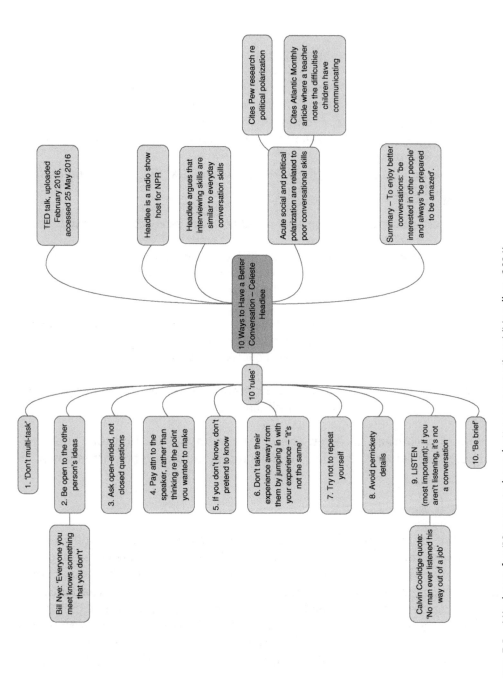

Figure 5.1 Mindmap for '10 ways to have better conversations' (Headlee, 2016)

key theorists' ideas, etc. Index cards may have an advantage over notebook notes as they can be shuffled into different orders which may help you structure your thinking when preparing to write your essay.

Note-taking using computer software

There are a number of proprietary programs or free open source software, such as Evernote (www.evernote.com), OneNote (www.onenote.com), GoogleKeep (www.google.com/keep/), Freemind (http://sourceforge.net/projects/freemind/) or Mindmup (www.mindmup.com) that are useful for note-taking, whether in a linear or mindmap form.

Note-taking using computer software has a few main advantages over paper-based notes:

- Foremost, perhaps, is that computer-based notes are searchable by keyword. This is incredibly helpful when you come to writing your essay.
- You can embed hyperlinks if you want to find your online source material quickly.
- You can cut and paste. This is great for speeding up referencing (you only have to type it correctly once!), or for copying over pithy quotes, including when you have noted an idea 'perfectly' in your own words.
- You can change and delete and add to your notes – and not end up with an unreadable mess. Chopping and changing must be done carefully, however, especially if you are mixing your own words with direct quotes from others, so as to avoid inadvertent plagiarism.
- When you are reading downloaded documents, you can also make marginal notes (depending on the file type) using track-changes.

One word of caution, however: anecdotally, many people find that handwritten notes are better at helping memory retention than typewritten notes.

Reference lists and citations

As part of your note-taking, you should ensure that you write down all of the sources you use – and where you found them. This is covered in detail in Chapter 10, which you may wish to glance at now. The important thing to remember is that referencing (acknowledgement of your sources) requires great care. You need to ensure your citations (precise notations of where your source material can be found) are accurate so that you can relocate your source material easily, and that once you have written your essay others (crucially, your tutor) can check or follow up on your work.

5.3 Academic literature searches and gathering data

You may have a set list of readings, particularly at the introductory levels of study, that your tutor has advised you to read in preparation for writing your essay. If this is the case, you may not need to look elsewhere for ideas or information. However, even if you are given a set reading list, it is as well to be familiar with what constitutes 'academic literature' and the process of gathering data. There are many books that introduce academic literature searching, and 'methodology' books that can tell you about how to collect and analyse existing, or 'secondary', data or how to develop your own 'primary' data. It is not the purpose of this book to replace the more detailed advice you can find in such texts – however, having an awareness of the process, and developing your skills as a social scientist will help you enormously when you come to write essays. For this reason, we have provided a short summary of what's involved.

Academic literature searches

In short, a literature search means browsing the writing that *already exists* in your field of study. But it is also more than this, because at the end of a literature search you should have:

- knowledge of the broad field of research in the area;
- understanding of the main theories, concepts and debates that have shaped the field;
- knowledge of more specific research and theorizing on your chosen topic;
- a set of notes on what you have found;
- a list of key theorists and their ideas, as well as counter-ideas;
- a set of appropriately tagged bookmarks (on Tagpacker – www.tagpacker.com, or Diigo – www.diigo.com, for instance);
- a full and accurate set of references (organized in BibMe – www.bibme.org, EndNote Basic – http://endnote.com, or Zotero – www.zotero.org, for instance).

The extent of your literature search will depend on a number of factors, most especially how much time you have.

We will consider the joys and perils of using online resources such as Wikipedia (http://wikipedia.org) in a moment. Let's assume, though, that you have looked up your topics in Wikipedia, so you have a baseline of non-peer-reviewed (we'll come back to this) information about your set topic. Now we'll look at more traditional social science resources. These come in a number of different forms: single author 'monographs', edited collections, journal articles, conference papers, official government or NGO (non-governmental organization) publications, or statistical websites and reference books.

Some books are 'textbooks' – in other words, they are specifically designed to be useful for teaching and are written for a novice readership. In these you will find overviews of main topics or theories. The most basic of these are titles like *Sociology for Beginners* (Osborne and Brew, 2016), or at a higher level *Understanding Foucault: A Critical Introduction* (Schirato et al., 2012). If you are in your first year or so of university, these sorts of texts can be immensely useful. But you will be able to tell by the slimness of the volume, the slow pace of explanations, or the lack of original writing (namely not the original author of the ideas presented) that these will not be *as* helpful to you later on in your studies, nor are they adequate for more in-depth research on a particular subject. So how do you find the 'right' kind of book, conference paper or journal article? The simple answer here is: go to your university library.

When searching the university's library catalogue, you will need to be adept at focusing your research on particular topics. Identifying the content words in your essay question is a good place to start (see Chapter 4).

Overview: Sources of information

Use the following to remind yourself of key resources and how you might use them.

Course reading list:
- Books:

  - I have found some of the books on the reading list and looked at them …
  - Contents pages:

    - I have looked for a word from the assignment question in the Contents pages.
    - I have chosen which sections of the book(s) to read.
    - I have gauged how much time I will need to read and take notes on these sections.

  - Indexes:

    - I have looked for the word in the Index at the back of the book.
    - I have looked at these pages and decided I will/will not read more of that book.

Wider searches:
- I have used the electronic catalogue in my library [and conducted] … key word, author or subject searches.
- I have used the following search engines or bookmarking networks: …
- I have asked the following people for assistance:

- ○ my tutor
- ○ other students
- ○ the subject librarian, who has directed me to:

  - ▪ these search engines ...
  - ▪ these journals/online journals ...
  - ▪ these websites for my subject.

- ○ my online study network

(Adapted from: Burns, T. and Sinfield, S. (2008) *Essential Study Skills*, London/Thousand Oaks, Sage, pp. 157–8.)

As you expand your searches beyond the recommended reading on your set lists, an important part of your task will be to ensure that the material you look at is credible. There are techniques for determining this. Your tutor will have done some of the work for you and you can assume that the readings on your recommended reading lists are credible; likewise, you can assume that the authors your tutor refers to most often, or those most cited within your set texts, are worth reading. But beyond this, you will need to rely on the shared conventions of the social sciences academy.

Peer review

You may have heard the phrase 'peer reviewed'. This simply means that a journal article or conference paper has been subject to scrutiny by other academics in the same subject area as the author of the article or paper. Although there are debates about the impact of the peer review system on innovation and debate in academia, it is generally seen as the best way to ensure that research is rigorous and that academic claims are well-argued and well-supported (see for instance, www.timeshighereducation.co.uk/story.asp?sectioncode=26&storycode=412600). Your tutor will likely guide you mostly towards peer-reviewed articles – and when you do your own searches, you should prioritize peer-reviewed sources.

Gathering data

Academic literature searches involve looking at what other people have written and researched. When you come to write about their research, it becomes 'secondary' material – in other words, you are reporting on it 'second hand' as you did not do the research yourself. Primary data, on the other hand, are data that you yourself have created. This might take the form of an interview, a content analysis, or a close reading of a film clip, etc. Where an essay question asks for examples or illustrative material, you should clarify with your tutor whether these should be examples researched or cited by others, or whether you should conduct your own research. Part of the purpose of doing a literature search is to see if anyone else has already done the research you are embarking on. If they have, it could be that your primary research will add weight to their argument; conversely, it could be that your research will throw into question some of the existing findings. Or it could be that social circumstances have changed and that what was claimed before no longer holds true. Knowing what empirical data have already been published, and what claims about it have already been made, will shape the kind of research – or primary data creation – you choose to do.

The perils of using the internet

'Wikipedia is a curse to higher education'. Discuss.

As far as we know this hasn't been set as an essay title, but perhaps it should be. Many tutors despair at finding references to Wikipedia in their students' essays, in part because Wikipedia is not a peer-reviewed source and the material posted to it can be unreliable or inaccurate. Worse is when students don't reference Wikipedia, and yet it is obvious that it has been a main source of material for an essay. Worse still, however, is the use of non-referenced articles or even whole essays which are available on the internet. In Chapter 12, we discuss the problems with plagiarism and how to avoid it, but for now we will focus on what is particularly problematic about using material from non-academic internet websites, such as Wikipedia:

- Material is not peer-reviewed in the traditional academic sense and risks therefore being inaccurate or academically unsound in other ways.
- Much Wikipedia material is itself unreferenced, so students can end up drawing on a range of resources of which they are wholly unaware. A plagiarism case where the student had copied a single page from Wikipedia revealed nine separate original resources, none of which were referenced on the Wikipedia site – nor, of course, in the student's essay.
- It is 'too easy' to cut and paste content, and simply forget to re-write in your own words or to reference. This practice may be an acceptable way to bring together information in some primary and secondary schools, but is not acceptable in higher education.
- The internet is vast – and without careful planning it is tremendously easy to waste a great deal of time on erroneous searches, or in being distracted by interesting but irrelevant material.

The pleasures of using the internet

On the other hand, the internet *is* vast and provides access to a wealth of excellent social science resources. It is essential to become adept at using the internet for academic purposes, including making good use of search engines, such as Google Scholar (http://scholar.google.co.uk), shared book-marking sites like Diigo (www.diigo.com), or tools like RSS feeds (which route updates from selected sites directly to your email). Becoming a social scientist also means making good use of research and academic networks in your subject area and amongst your student colleagues. This may mean subscribing to your tutor's blog, or to recommended blogs by experts in your field, or to relevant social and academic networking sites. Increasingly, tutors will expect students to collaborate on some assessments, using sharing tools like DropBox or wikis that enable students to comment on each others' work, or even add, change or delete group project material. This 'atelier' approach to interactive, peer group learning can be facilitated by a range of online software.

Your university is likely to make use of a VLE (virtual learning environment), such as Moodle (http://moodle.org) for teaching and learning, and this may have in-built resources such as referencing tools, wikis or forums. Where your university has its own bespoke platform and tools, you would be advised to use these (although it is increasingly easy to share across platforms).

If you have mainly used the internet for informal learning or social networking, you may find it helpful to learn a bit more about using it for research. Your university library may have its own set of online learning tools, or you might look at MOOCs (massively open online courses), such as those on FutureLearn, for specific short courses on using the internet for formal learning.

Summary

- Purposeful and active reading, which involves being able to scan material quickly, as well as reading in-depth and critically, is essential to good essay writing.
- Note-taking is part of active reading and helps you remember what you have read. It is also essential for helping you to see what material you have and what further material you will need to write your essay. Note-taking is a 'personal thing': linear or diagrammatic notes are both fine.
- You should make use of sources recommended by your tutor and focus on peer-reviewed journals when conducting independent research.

(Continued)

(Continued)

- Primary data are data created and reported by the original researcher.
- Secondary data are data that are reported second hand.
- Internet sources may not be credible and special caution should be used when cutting and pasting from online materials.
- Internet sources may be excellent and can expand your network of colleagues and subject knowledge.
- You would be wise to develop your online learning skills, using relevant software (such as note-taking, bookmarking, referencing and social learning tools).

Self-test

1 What sorts of questions can help you read 'analytically and critically'?
2 What are the advantages of taking notes on a computer? By hand?
3 Why do you think you should prioritize 'peer-reviewed' academic journal articles?
4 What are some of the risks associated with using material downloaded from the internet?

Don't forget! Visit **https://study.sagepub.com/redmanandmaples5** for more tasks and resources related to this chapter.

6

Thinking Critically and Formulating an Argument

- Critical thinking
- Formulating an argument

Much of this book focuses on relatively straightforward work you can do to improve your writing. Accurate citations, helpful notes, essay planning and a clear structure to your essay can make a big difference to your marks. However, in order to gain the top grades in any social science subject, you will need to develop your critical thinking skills and ability to formulate an argument. This is something that will take time and effort – but if you are after top marks, it will be worth it.

6.1 Critical thinking

Chapter 2 (section 2.2) introduced you to the circuit of knowledge, which is a useful tool for thinking critically as a social scientist. Although some social science ideas and theories can be complex, the basic point of thinking like a social scientist is to consider the usefulness (strengths and weaknesses) of evidence and the power (logic, explanatory reach) of concepts, arguments and theories in making sense of our social world.

As we've discussed, you should approach your reading critically – for instance, to consider whether an author is making a convincing argument, whether there is a logic or 'sense' to it, and whether the evidence being cited adequately supports the claims made. When taking notes you might try to compare one argument with another, or think about whether there are other issues or explanations that could be considered. When writing, an important part of your work will involve organizing your thoughts into a logical order, making coherent arguments that are backed up with sound evidence, and being attuned to any bias or preconceptions you might bring to your studies. In short, at every stage of your work, you should be engaged in critical thinking. But how can you do this?

In section 5.1 we looked at 'interrogating' your reading – asking a series of questions that will help you to understand the material more deeply. The circuit of knowledge (section 2.2) points up the importance of concepts and theories, and the use of evidence. Here we consider how to *judge* the evidence you select, and the arguments you make, using a simple set of criteria:

- Validity
- Reliability
- Comprehensiveness
- Coherence.

In general, validity and reliability refer to the usefulness of evidence, and comprehensiveness and coherence refer to the strength of concepts, arguments and theories.

Validity

'Validity' describes the degree to which data (evidence) measure or represent what they claim to measure or represent. Hugh MacKay and Paul Reynolds give this example:

> ... to test the hypothesis that mobile telephones, e-mail and other new communication technologies mean that we keep in closer touch with family and friends, we need to establish a direct relationship between use of the new technology and greater or closer contact with family and friends. It is not enough to claim a change in communication technology and to demonstrate an increased volume of use, and then to assume that this means that we keep in touch with family and friends more because, for instance, we might be contacting not family and friends but people we hardly know. (2001, pp. 49–50)

Reliability

Is the evidence you are citing specific to a particular time, date, group of people – or would the same results occur at a different time, on a different day, with a different group? To put it in the terms of the natural sciences, if an experiment were repeated would it get the same results? If the answer is 'yes', then you can claim that the data are 'reliable'. Unfortunately, social science doesn't often afford the same control over variables that natural science does – in other words, it is difficult to replicate social science research exactly, time and again, because people and their social-environmental contexts change.

Comprehensiveness

'Comprehensiveness' describes the 'reach' of a claim. If we were to claim that 'there has been an increase in the use of doorstep grocery deliveries', we would need to clarify whether this is the case in both urban and rural areas, amongst men and women, wealthy and poor, and older and younger shoppers. If we find that all of these categories of shoppers have increased their use of doorstep grocery delivery, we can say that this is a comprehensive assertion – in other words, there is significant reach to the claim. Limited comprehensiveness is not a problem however: the problem is claiming a greater comprehensiveness than there is evidence for.

Coherence

Is there a logic to the argument or claim, or are there inconsistencies or flaws in the argument, the concepts used, or the assumptions behind the argument? Put in a slightly different way, we might think, as David Goldblatt does, about 'testing' accounts of society. He identifies three key features:

- The clarity of key claims and concepts
- The logic of the chain of reasoning
- The plausibility and accuracy of the hidden assumptions behind the claims and reasoning.

(Adapted from: Goldblatt, D. (2000), cited in Mackay, H. et al. (2001), *Social Science in Action: Investigating the Information Society*, Milton Keynes/London, The Open University/Routledge, p. 51.)

Implicit in these considerations is self-reflection. Thinking critically involves taking the time to reflect on what you *think* you have learned, and asking yourself (using the tests above, the circuit of knowledge, ideas that have come up in tutorials, or discussions with other students) whether it makes sense *to you*. You should also test out your ideas with fellow students – discussing ideas with others is crucial to developing your own understanding.

6.2 Formulating an argument

How to formulate an argument brings us back to the circuit of knowledge and draws on your skills of critical thinking. Where you have been given an essay question, your argument will, to some extent, be determined for you. As section 2.2 and Chapter 4 point out, answering the question as set is essential: but what if you have only been given a broad topic about which to write? In this case you might be asking 'How do I work out what to say?', and the question of how to formulate an argument becomes all the more pressing.

How do I work out what I want to say?

Without giving too pat an answer to this, one tried and tested way of developing your ideas about a social science topic is to focus on what cultural theorist Stuart Hall (and others) identified as 'the differences that make a difference' (Hall, 1992, 1997). These include race, ethnicity, gender, sexuality, class, age, etc. These differences throw up issues of disparity, inequality, or contingencies between groups. Other 'matters that matter' might include urban or rural locations, cities or towns, employment, access to technologies, access to health services, marital status, or the wealth or poverty of individuals or groups or their home nations.

You should be pragmatic about your focus. You will need to make use of the material presented on your module, and consider your tutor's areas of interest, in determining the issues that will inform or shape your essay. In addition, you will need to gauge whether you have time to find sufficient material on your chosen topic and if that material is easily accessible. This doesn't mean you should always choose 'safe' subjects – just that you should be realistic about what can be achieved in the given time.

Often, this means narrowing your focus.

Let's say you are taking a module on 'Women and Technology' and your tutor has set a 2,000-word essay around women and mobile technologies. Looking at the set reading, you find material on women and mobile, or cell, phones, but little on women and laptops or tablets. Also, the readings mainly cite research conducted in the USA and Australia, and less on developing nations. The obvious essay would compare men's and women's use of cell phones in the USA and whether these uses have changed over time. But narrowing your focus could result in a more interesting essay. You might compare Australian and US women's uptake of mobile phones, comparing the different speeds and distribution of their uptake across different social and economic variables (rural vs urban adoption; women in paid vs unpaid employment; women with/without children, etc.). Alternatively, you could consider whether women's use of cell phones is different depending on age, again drawing in other social variables such as wealth/poverty, pre-existing social networks, or other experiences with technologies. Hopefully you can see that the 'differences that make a difference' have informed these suggestions.

Once you have your topic, you should now – effectively – set yourself an essay question. Throughout this book we introduce various sorts of essay question, and in sections 4.2 and 4.3 we looked at how different types of questions are intended to test different sorts of knowledge and skills. This is something you can consider when developing your own question. Will it be 'enough' to ask for a straightforward description? Will your tutor expect you to be able to evaluate evidence, or two (or more) competing theories at this stage in your studies? Has there been much emphasis on independent reading, or are you expected to make full use only of the set texts? At undergraduate level there is generally less expectation that you will produce original research or thinking in your work. There is, however, also an expectation that you will be able to utilize the original thinking of others in putting together a coherent essay. You should, increasingly, be able to present the research findings of others correctly, and provide appropriate context so that your reader can understand the significance of any findings. These are considerations that you will need to make in creating your own essay question.

Taking one of the examples above – women's use of mobile phones depending on age – we could come up with a range of essay questions, some more appropriate at earlier stages of study, some testing more advanced skills:

- Identify the key differences in the use of mobile phones for women in the 18–25 and 50–65 age ranges. (1,000 words)
- Explain some of the key reasons why the use of mobile phones may differ between women of 18–25 and those in the 50–65 age range. (1,500 words)
- 'Mobile phone use is core to younger women's identities, more so than for older women.' Evaluate this claim. (2,000 words)

There is a clear progression of skills and word limits in these examples. The first example requires simple description, and whilst you might be tempted to make comparisons this is not an explicit requirement. The second asks for more information: in order to 'explain', you would need first to state the differences and provide some reasons why those differences exist. Here you are implicitly required to compare. The third is certainly the most difficult as it requires some description of the various uses of mobile phones, as well as some explanation, but more than this there is a requirement to consider both the merits of any evidence and explore theories of identity (and technology).

Formulating an argument begins with a question – which brings us back to the circuit of knowledge. Excepting *purely* descriptive essays, you will next consider claims, such as those to do with disparities, inequalities or contingencies. Concepts and theories help us consider the evidence we might find. Completing the circuit of knowledge, we evaluate the evidence, theories and concepts we've used, and then perhaps re-interrogate the question. It is essential for your essay that this occurs in a logical sequence, with each point building on or developing the previous point.

Summary

- Thinking critically is essential in social science work and will help you achieve higher marks.
- Critical thinking is something you should do actively whilst reading and note-taking and should be demonstrated in your essay writing, particularly at intermediate and advanced levels.
- There are four simple criteria you can use to judge the usefulness of evidence and the power of concepts, arguments and theories. These are validity, reliability, comprehensiveness, and coherence.
- Validity – the data presented measure what they claim to measure.
- Reliability – if repeated under the same conditions, the 'experiment' will yield the same results. This is difficult for social science, as social conditions change and are not easily controlled.
- Comprehensiveness – the 'reach' of a theory or claim. It is fine to have limited comprehensiveness, provided you identify the scope of your claim.
- Coherence – the logic of an argument or theory, and the assumptions behind an argument or theory.
- Critical thinking is a reflective process.
- Deciding what to write about in the social sciences can often be guided by the 'differences that make a difference' or the 'matters that matter'.
- Formulating an argument requires careful ordering in a logical sequence – the circuit of knowledge can help identify the development of points in an argument.
- Developing your own essay question should involve consideration of your level of study, and the sorts of skills and knowledge you think your tutor is interested in testing.

Self-test

1 What are validity and reliability concerned with?
2 What are comprehensiveness and coherence concerned with?
3 What are the 'differences that make a difference'?
4 How might you make a broad area of inquiry into a social science question?
5 How might you make an area of inquiry into a more challenging social science question?

Don't forget! Visit **https://study.sagepub.com/redmanandmaples5** for more tasks and resources related to this chapter.

7

Writing Introductions

- Longer or 'full' introductions
- Basic short introductions
- When do you write the introduction?

There are of course many ways to write an essay introduction. In this chapter we will be exploring one of these – an approach that treats the introduction like an 'abstract' or brief synopsis of the central points raised in the essay, and 'signposts' what you intend to say. The introduction-as-synopsis will cover just about everything that an effective introduction should achieve and will do this using a minimum number of words – an important consideration when the number of words available to you is limited. Having mastered this style of introduction, you will probably want to move on to writing introductions that are more creative.

You should not, therefore, feel obliged to follow these guidelines slavishly. Indeed, there is a danger that too rigid an interpretation of the advice in this chapter will cause your introductions to become dry and formulaic. As such they may fail to grab your reader's attention. Academic writers often attempt to avoid this problem by, for example, beginning an article or chapter with an arresting quotation, image or challenging statement. Alternatively, they may start with a short discussion of an example or theme central to the matter in hand, and use this to raise or signpost the questions to be addressed in the work that follows.

You may want to look for these and similar strategies in your reading. You might also wish to check the length of introductions. A general rule is that the introduction should account for between 5 and 10 per cent of the overall word count – but you will notice that in professional academic writing there is some considerable variation.

As with other areas of essay writing, you will probably find that you get better at introductions the more experienced you become. It is certainly fair to say that essays set at more advanced levels will expect more from your introductions than those at the introductory level. An introductory-level essay should be able to identify its subject and begin to highlight key themes or arguments. More advanced essays should display a firm grasp of the central debates that lie 'behind' the question, and provide a more sophisticated indication of the arguments it will develop. Sometimes more advanced essays will also need to 'establish a position' in the introduction, indicating that they are being written from 'within' a particular theory or perspective. This chapter explores these issues by looking at:

- longer or 'full' introductions for essays over 1,500 words;
- basic short introductions for essays under 1,500 words.

7.1 Longer or 'full' introductions

With longer essays, introductions can be written as a section in their own right and may well be several paragraphs long. 'Full' introductions generally do most or all of the following: identify the subject of the essay; signpost the shape and content of the argument; highlight the major debates that lie 'behind' the question; define terms; and (sometimes) establish a position. We will consider each of these features in more detail below.

Identifying the subject of the essay

The easiest way to do this is to refer back to the question. Let's take an example from popular culture (for examples treated in more depth, see the full essays in Chapter 14). For instance, if the essay question asks you to 'Evaluate the claim that *Coronation Street* is the most enjoyable contemporary British soap opera', you may want to write:

> This essay will evaluate the claim that *Coronation Street* is the most enjoyable contemporary British soap opera.

However, you can always be more creative than this, provided what you write is relevant. For example, you might write:

> *Coronation Street* consistently receives high viewer ratings. This essay explores the basis of this popularity, evaluating its appeal in comparison with *EastEnders*, one of its major ratings rivals.

Signposting the shape of the argument

The intention here is to give the reader a 'road map' of the essay. At its simplest this involves highlighting the main stages of your argument. For instance, you might write:

> The first section focuses on … This argument is developed in the following section, which compares …

Identifying the sequence and shape of your argument in this manner is called 'signposting', and it is an important technique that you can deploy throughout an essay.

Highlighting major debates and signposting the content of the argument

Essay questions will often centre on a key debate or debates: for example, 'Do the wealthier Western nations exploit the poorer nations?' or 'Is behaviour biologically or socially produced?' Often these debates will not be referred to explicitly but will lie 'behind' or be implied in the question. Your introduction will need to pull out these debates and signpost your essay's responses to them. This will form the core of your argument. For instance, in the *Coronation Street* example, it may be possible to argue that, historically, the show has emphasized a less naturalistic style than *EastEnders*, one that is characterized by strong female characters and comic men. With this in mind, it might be that one of the debates lying 'behind' the question centres on the issue of whether *Coronation Street*'s less naturalistic style is more appealing to certain audiences, or whether people are more drawn to the much-vaunted 'gritty realism' of *EastEnders*. In order to refer to this debate, your introduction could be re-written to look like this:

> *Coronation Street* consistently receives high viewer ratings. This essay explores the basis of this popularity, evaluating its appeal in comparison with *EastEnders*, one of its major ratings rivals. In the process, the essay will analyse *Coronation Street*'s use of strong female characters, its exploration of women's lives, and its often humorous treatment of men, contrasting these to the 'gritty realism' of its competitor show.

You will see that this introduction not only draws attention to the possible difference in style between *Coronation Street* and *EastEnders* (a debate lying 'behind' the question), but also suggests that its appeal lies in particular features of the show: strong women characters, its exploration of women's lives, and the humorous treatment of men. In other words, the introduction signposts these as central components of the essay's argument.

Defining terms

People can be over-enthusiastic about defining terms, so don't feel you have to define absolutely everything. Nevertheless, definitions can be useful in relation to the following:

- Key concepts and obviously technical terms

For example, if you are asked to assess critically a particular concept or theory (say, the notion of inequality, the cultural imperialism thesis, or cognitive developmental theory), it is fairly obvious that you will need to provide a definition or outline of it. In fact, it may be that this definition or outline will require several sentences and will look over-long and clumsy if included with your other introductory remarks. In consequence, you may decide that it is more appropriate to allot it a section of its own, perhaps immediately after the introduction proper.

- Terms that are contested

For instance, the question 'Is the family in Britain in crisis?' hinges upon how you define 'crisis'. For some people factors such as the rising post-war divorce rate, increased numbers of single-parent families, and the increasing profile of feminism and lesbian and gay relationships constitute a 'crisis'. Other people find these developments positive or less problematic. Here you would need to point to the contested nature of the term, and highlight the fact that it is open to competing definitions.

- Theories or approaches that have different versions

Particularly on more advanced university courses where there is a greater emphasis on theoretical complexity, you will need to define the particular version of the theory or approach that you are using. For example, it may not be enough to say that you will use a perspective informed by psychoanalytic theory or feminist theory, since there are competing versions of both. You may choose to align your argument with that of a particular theorist, or even a selected work by a particular theorist. You can do this in two main ways: by naming the theorist, and more convincingly, by making accurate use of the sorts of terminology he or she uses (part of 'writing from within a perspective' – see section 8.2).

Establishing a position

Establishing a position means indicating the particular 'line' you intend to take in an essay. The statement 'This essay explores the use of capital punishment in the USA' certainly tells us what the essay is about. However, the statement 'This essay explores the use of capital punishment in the USA and argues that it is a fundamental abuse of human rights' clearly establishes the author's position on this issue, and anticipates or signals the content of the essay's conclusion. This helps orient the reader towards the essay's argument, and ensures that the main point is lodged in her or his mind.

What would our *Coronation Street* example look like if we included a statement that identified our position? Perhaps something like this:

> *Coronation Street* consistently receives high viewer ratings. This essay explores the basis of this popularity, evaluating its appeal in comparison with *EastEnders*, one of its major ratings rivals. In its opening section, the essay uses a feminist analysis to argue that *Coronation Street*'s appeal may be found in its 'women-centredness', in particular its focus on strong female characters, its exploration of women's lives, and its often humorous treatment of men. The essay then goes on to explore the contrasting approach adopted in *EastEnders*, which has often focused on social issues and emphasized a 'gritty realism'. The essay argues that, in comparison to *Coronation Street*, this 'gritty realism' fails to connect with women's culture, and that it is the appeal to women of these less naturalistic elements that underlies *Coronation Street*'s continuing popularity.

The 'position' established here is a feminist one, although we haven't indicated what form of feminism this might be. A more advanced introduction might include a nod to Christine Geraghty or Charlotte Brunsdon who have written on the positive significance of soaps as feminist texts: 'In its opening section, the essay draws on Geraghty (1991) for a feminist analysis of the television programme, arguing that *Coronation Street*'s appeal may be found in its "women-centredness", in particular … '.

An alternative structure for the full introduction

Full introductions will signpost the content of each section of the essay. A straightforward way of doing this is to list the sections in the order in which they appear, as above. Alternatively, you may wish to indicate the broad order of the essay, emphasizing the most significant arguments, but at the end of your introduction say what you will be doing next:

Coronation Street consistently receives high viewer ratings and this essay explores the basis of this popularity. The essay argues that *Coronation Street*'s appeal may be found in its 'women-centredness', in particular its focus on strong female characters, its exploration of women's lives, and its often humorous treatment of men. The essay then goes on to explore the contrasting approach adopted in *EastEnders*, one of its main ratings rivals, which has often focused on social issues and emphasized a 'gritty realism'. The essay argues that, in comparison to *Coronation Street*, this 'gritty realism' fails to connect with women's culture, and that it is the appeal to women of these less naturalistic elements that underlies *Coronation Street*'s continuing popularity. First, however, the essay considers Dorothy Hobson's (1982) analysis of the importance of ritual engagement with television programmes such as soap operas.

7.2 Basic short introductions

In a very short essay, you may only have between 50 and 150 words to tell your reader what the essay is about. As a result, your introduction will need to be concise and highly focused. However, it should still:

- identify the subject of the essay and define key terms;
- highlight any major debates that lie 'behind' the question;
- signpost the essay's key argument(s).

Thus a short introduction to the question 'Evaluate the claim that *Coronation Street* is the most enjoyable contemporary British soap opera' might read more like one of our earlier versions, for example:

> *Coronation Street* consistently receives high viewer ratings. This essay explores the basis of this popularity, evaluating its appeal in comparison with ratings rival *EastEnders*. The essay will analyse *Coronation Street*'s use of strong female characters, its exploration of women's lives, and its often humorous treatment of men, contrasting these to the 'gritty realism' of its competitor show.

Outlining the content of your core argument will alert your reader to what is most important about the essay or what makes it 'hang together'. You may notice that the sequence signposts have changed in this shorter version. This will not always be the case, but you may find that when you strip down your work to its bare bones, the emphasis of the argument will change – as has happened here.

The difference between an introductory level introduction and one that is at a more advanced level is somewhat nuanced, however, at the more advanced level the vernacular of the field – including background themes and debates – will be skilfully deployed, while at introductory level it is expected that introductions will be more descriptive and less steeped in the language and background of the subject area. Intermediate-level essays will make proficient use of key terms, and may move towards indicating the background issues and debates that will have shaped the essay question.

Turn to Essay 3, Chapter 14. This provides an example of a formal social science essay. Read the introduction and answer yes or no.

- Can you see the different elements described above?
- Has the introduction told the reader what the essay is about?
- Has it provided a synopsis of the key points?
- Has it indicated any 'underlying debates'?
- Has it indicated the structure of the essay?
- Do you think this is a good introduction?
- Could it be improved?

Now turn to Essay 4's introduction. What would you change to make it stronger?

7.3 When do you write the introduction?

The difficulty with introduction writing is that sometimes you will only know how the core arguments have developed when you have finished your essay. So although writing the introduction can help give you a clearer idea of what you plan to do, and in what order, you will find it is better to finalize your introduction once the rest of the essay is complete.

Summary

- The introduction tells the reader what your essay is about and gives an indication of the order in which your arguments will appear.
- An introduction should normally constitute between 5 and 10 per cent of the essay's total length.
- There is more than one way to write an introduction. The approach adopted here treats the introduction as an 'abstract' or synopsis of key points.

(Continued)

(Continued)

- A 'full' introduction: identifies the subject of the essay; signposts the shape of the argument; highlights the major debates that lie 'behind' the question; signposts the content of the argument; (where necessary) defines terms; (sometimes) establishes a position, or looks ahead to the conclusion.
- A basic short introduction should tell the reader what the essay is about by: identifying the subject of the essay; highlighting the major debates that lie 'behind' the question; and identifying the essay's key argument(s) or theme(s).
- An introduction written to 'introductory' standards should be proficient at identifying the subject of the essay, and signposting the shape of the argument.
- An introduction written to an 'intermediate' standard should move towards highlighting the major debates raised by the essay question; signposting the content of the argument; (if necessary) defining terms effectively; and (if appropriate) establishing a position.
- An introduction written to an 'advanced' standard should show greater sophistication in bringing out the major debates raised by the question; signposting the content of the argument; (if necessary) defining terms; and (if appropriate) establishing a position.
- Essays 1 and 3 in Chapter 14 illustrate stronger introductions. Essays 2 and 4 in Chapter 14 illustrate weaker introductions.
- You may choose to write your introduction first to give you an idea of what you intend to do with your essay, but you are likely to produce a more accurate introduction once you have completed the main sections and conclusion.

Self-test

1 What are the components of a full introduction?
2 What is signposting and why is it important to the reader?
3 What, at minimum, should a short or basic introduction do?
4 What are some of the differences between introductory-, intermediate-, and advanced-level essays?
5 When should you write the introduction?

Don't forget! Visit **https://study.sagepub.com/redmanandmaples5** for more tasks and resources related to this chapter.

8

Writing the Main Section

- Structuring your argument
- Using evidence to support your argument
- Adding weight to your argument
- Communicating your argument

Before you begin drafting your main section you may find it helpful to look back at Chapter 4, particularly the guidance on how to make your essay address appropriately the type of question you are answering. You may also want to review Chapter 6, particularly section 6.2 on formulating an argument.

8.1 Structuring your argument

Your essay will need a strong and coherent structure if you are to convince the reader of your case. Central to this is the process of building an argument (that is, making each point follow on from the previous one). It has been claimed that creating a logical progression to a social scientific argument is not dissimilar to the way we argue in everyday life. In the example below, we imagine a series of points advocating home cooking that may be made in a discussion about whether it is better to cook at home, or to have a meal out with friends:

'I think it is usually better to have friends over and to cook for them at home.'

'You can decide what to have on the day, and you don't have to book for a particular time. And there's no problem about transport, or parking.'

'You can dress up for spag bol if you feel like it – or have fancy food in your pyjamas if you like.'

'Most of the time, homecooked food tastes better and is better for you. I don't use any cheap "substitute" ingredients, and I use a lot less salt and sugar in my recipes than they do in most restaurants. And you don't have to have standard portions – if someone wants a little or a lot, they can have a small portion or seconds.'

'I really like cooking, and I think it's nice to share new recipes with my friends.'

You might notice that this is similar to the kind of argument you would find in an introductory-level advocacy essay: there is limited scope for compare and contrast and little evaluation, but there is a logical progression that explains the author's position. If we break it down, it looks something like this:

- *Outlines a particular point of view*

'I think it is usually better to have friends over and to cook for them at home.'

- *Gives reasons for holding this view*

'You can decide what to have on the day ... don't have to book for a particular time ... there's no problem about transport, or parking ... you can dress up ... if you like ... homecooked food tastes better and is better for you ... you don't have to have standard portions ... it's nice to share new recipes with my friends.'

- *Gives evidence*

Homecooked food and cooking for friends are better because 'I don't use any cheap "substitute" ingredients and I use a lot less salt and sugar in my recipes than they do in most restaurants ... if someone wants a little or a lot, they can have a small portion or seconds'.

If you're the sort of person who likes diagrams, you can represent the stages of this process as in Figure 8.1.

You might suggest that there is considerable room for debate here – and you might also notice there are some implicit qualifiers throughout the argument above. For instance, problems with parking might be just as difficult near your or your friends' home as at a restaurant, and the author uses the phrases 'most of the time' and 'most restaurants', suggesting that home-cooked food isn't always better and some restaurants might use similar ingredients in their cooking. To make this a stronger argument, these debates and qualifiers would need to be addressed. To make this into an essay form, it would also, of course, need an introduction and a conclusion.

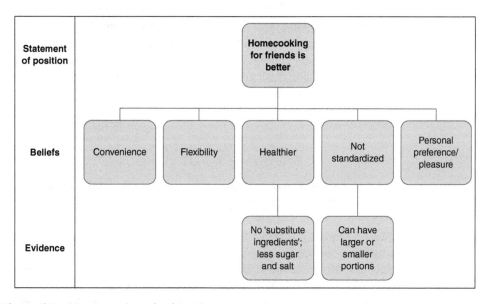

Figure 8.1 'Homecooking for friends versus going out to eat': logical progression arguing that homecooking is better

If you now turn to Essay 1 in Chapter 14, you will find an example of an essay that develops a logically progressing argument. Read the essay in its entirety and note down what you see as the main stages in its argument as you read.

If we 'strip down' the argument in Essay 1, we can see that it goes through the following stages:

1. It makes the claim that a social constructionist account is more persuasive than the alternative, biological account.
2. It identifies the reasons to support this view (for example, Butler's notion that sex/gender is a 'performative enactment'; Connell's argument that sex/gender is a relational category produced in a process of 'hegemonic' struggle).
3. It cites evidence from sociological and educational research literature on sex/gender and schooling to evaluate this argument.

A standard structure for an essay is an introduction, three main arguments or discussion points, with evidence to support these, and a conclusion.

The stages of the argument in Essay 1 are slightly more complicated than this: for instance, it uses Connell early on to question some aspects of the social constructionist case and then returns to these points in its conclusion. However, the basic structure can still be seen, as it were, beneath the surface of the essay. Depending on the essay question, the main body of a 1,500-word essay may have up to five or six key points. As the set lengths of your essays increase, you will probably find you are making more and more complex arguments, which may fall into the standard 'three main point' structure, or may require you to be more creative with organizing your thoughts. Looking at the structure of refereed journal articles or textbook chapters will more than often reveal these common 'essay' structures.

Summary

- The argument in the main section of an essay needs to have a 'logical progression'.
- We construct logically progressing arguments in everyday life.
- Logical progression in a social science essay involves: outlining a particular point of view; giving reasons why this point of view might be correct; and providing theoretical and empirical evidence to support these claims.
- A standard structure for an essay is an introduction, three main arguments or discussion points, and a conclusion. However, depending on the essay question, a 1,500-word essay may have up to five or six key points plus an introduction and conclusion. Academic journal articles generally follow standard essay structures.

8.2 Using evidence to support your argument

In section 2.2, it was argued that claims made in social science essays need to be supported by appropriate evidence. Indeed, more advanced undergraduate courses are likely to require you to draw on an increasing range of sources, including primary texts and other original material. Clearly, in handling this material, you will need to reorganize it in a way that answers the question. You will also need to select from it the evidence that most effectively supports your argument.

Selecting evidence – using a range of examples

Any essay question will expect you to support your arguments with appropriate examples and evidence. However, as you develop intermediate and advanced essay-writing skills, you will be expected to demonstrate an increasing ability to select examples that illustrate and support your points most effectively.

In general, you should:

- *Highlight examples that have the most significant or far-reaching implications.* These examples will need to be relevant to the question and engage with the point you are making. This means being selective. You cannot cite every single related example or piece of evidence in the relevant literature. Some examples will be more useful to your purpose than others, and you will need to identify these and relate them to the issue under discussion.
- *Where possible, support your argument with more than one example.* This does not mean that you should use a number of examples to make the same point over and over again. Rather, what is being suggested is that you will need to draw on a range of examples to illustrate the different aspects of your argument. However, you will sometimes need to decide whether it is more effective to explore an issue in greater depth or breadth. For instance, exploring one or a limited range of examples in depth may allow you to provide a richer and more detailed account than exploring a breadth of examples only briefly. You will need to decide which strategy is most appropriate according to the question and the material available.
- *Select examples from a range of sources.* Particularly on more advanced courses, you will need to look for a breadth of source material, thereby demonstrating your familiarity with the field. As well as the academic literature, it may be that up-to-the-minute examples can be found in, for example, news, current affairs, political blogs – or if you are studying an applied social science, or your course has a practical component, your own experience. Where such examples are effective in illuminating an argument they can be a useful addition to your essay.
- *Work from the general to the particular.* Specific examples should be used to support general arguments. Whereas a general argument cannot necessarily be induced from only one or two concrete examples, one or two concrete examples can be used to illustrate the plausibility of a general argument on the grounds that there are many more examples of the same point, but due to the limits of the word count and because you don't wish to be repetitive, it is not possible to cite them in your essay.

Turn again to Essay 1 in Chapter 14. What examples can you identify and how are these used?

As you will have seen, Essay 1 cites a range of examples from the research literature on sex/gender and schooling to support and illustrate what it identifies as the three major arguments to be found in this literature (that the content and practices of schooling encode sex/gender; that pupils actively use sex/gender to negotiate schooling; and that sex/gender relations intersect with other social relations in the school). It attempts to identify particularly 'rich' examples, to cite different sources, to indicate where similar data can be found in other research, and to work from the general to the particular.

Selecting evidence – using empirical evidence

In the preceding paragraphs we have explored, in general terms, the use of examples as evidence. However, it is important to be clear that these examples will frequently be drawn from concrete research findings. Social scientists carry out research in order to gather evidence to substantiate or falsify their theories and arguments. Evidence from such research is called empirical evidence (loosely speaking, evidence collected via systematic and rigorous observation), and since it comes from checkable, usually published investigation, it is more highly regarded than everyday examples or personal experience. As is the case with Essay 1, a good essay will use empirical evidence to support the arguments made. This involves more than simply describing relevant research findings. The task is to make clear exactly how these findings support or illustrate your arguments. For example, in Essay 1 you will find the following paragraph:

> As well as producing sex/gender through friendship group interactions, the literature also suggests that pupils use sex/gender to negotiate and resist schooling. Kehily and Nayak (1996, p. 214) describe an account from a group of secondary school pupils in which one of them (Samantha) was claimed to have pursued a teacher (Mr Smedley) round the classroom with a sprig of mistletoe with the intention of 'getting some lipstick on the top of his head'. In this instance, a hetero-sexualized form of femininity is used satirically to undermine the authority of a male teacher (see also Walkerdine, 1981).

This paragraph:

- identifies the argument (that the social meanings and practices of sex/gender are used by pupils to negotiate and resist schooling);
- cites research evidence to support this claim (from Kehily and Nayak, 1996);
- explains exactly how this evidence illustrates the initial argument (it is an instance where heterosexual femininity was used to undermine a male teacher's authority);
- provides an additional reference indicating further research findings supporting this argument (Walkerdine, 1981).

Selecting evidence – using maps, diagrams and numerical data

Maps, diagrams and numerical data are further major sources of evidence that you can use to illustrate and support an argument. Rather like quotations, maps, diagrams and numerical data should be used to illustrate and support key points and not to replace them, so always remember to integrate them: don't make them 'stand alone'. In addition, remember that maps, tables and graphs are not hard facts. You will need to be critical of your numerical sources by, for example, bearing in mind what scale is being used and how this shapes the evidence, by questioning how data have been collected, or by asking how a graph would change if plotted over a wider timescale. You should also be aware that numerical data represent specific outcomes, and that the underlying causes of those outcomes will be unclear and will need further investigation. For example, it is quite possible for different combinations of causes to produce a similar numerical outcome.

Table 8.1 'Visits abroad by UK residents', in thousands

	North America	Europe	of which EU	Other countries	Total world	Percent change
Annual						
2006	4,702	55,170	51,314	9,664	69,536	3.4
2007	4,587	55,188	51,186	9,675	69,450	−0.1
2008	4,629	54,424	50,081	9,958	69,011	−0.6
2009	3,652	45,944	42,396	9,018	58,614	−15.1
2010	3,653	42,565	38,925	9,344	55,562	−5.2
2011	3,668	44,065	40,487	9,103	56,836	2.3
2012	3,394	44,217	40,777	8,926	56,538	−0.5
2013	3,389	45,319	41,958	9,085	57,792	2.2
2014	3,677	47,025	43,834	9,380	60,082	4.0
2015	3,912	51,743	48,113	10,065	65,720	9.4

Office for National Statistics (2016a)

In this case, the data are from the UK's Office of National Statistics, which is generally considered to be a reliable source. However, we might want to know what sorts of visits are included in these data (holidays or business travel, flights, cruises or train travel – in fact, the data include all of these) and which methods were used to produce these figures (the ONS publishes information on its methodologies: see www.ons.gov.uk/methodology/methodologytopicsandstatisticalconcepts).

What can we see from the table? Broadly, UK residents' travel abroad decreased from 2006 to 2015, but 2009 and 2010 show significant depreciations in overseas travel. In reading the data, of course, we need to be careful not to infer causation from correlation, but we might be tempted to speculate about a relationship between a decline in overseas travel and the 2008 economic crash. From these data, however, we can say only that there has been a decrease in overseas visits by UK residents since 2006, and that this decrease appears to have been significant (–15.1%) in 2009.

What further evidence might alter our perception of this change? Note that the timescale covers only a single decade: we can imagine that the figures for travel abroad would have been very different in the 1980s – or 1950s, or 1920s (due to population differences, of course, but also the availability and affordability of different forms of transport). Looking at a thirty-year time-span (1986–2016), the data suggest the broader trend is for an increase in overseas travel (see Figure 8.2) and that the 2009–2010 decrease marks a relatively small 'blip'.

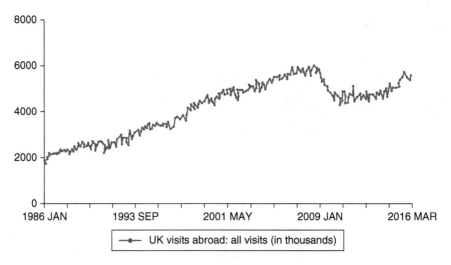

Figure 8.2   'UK visits abroad: all visits, January 1986 to March 2016'

Office for National Statistics (2016b).

We might also change our interpretation of travel trends by looking at the countries visited in more detail. Table 8.2 covers a much shorter time period (2011–2015), but gives information about visits to (some) individual countries, which could be revealing.

Can you make sense of the increased/decreased travel to Brazil between 2011 and 2015? How about Egypt? (See Figures 8.3 and 8.4.)

Again, however, it is important not to infer too much, nor to assume data are relevant for all time. The map of Egypt was current on 29 May 2016, but the UK government's foreign travel advice will certainly have changed since then.

Table 8.2   Number of visits abroad by UK residents by main country visited, in thousands, 2011–2015 (abridged)

	Visits (thousands)					Average annual growth 2011–15 (%)
	2011	2012	2013	2014	2015	
Canada	437	382	364	420	410	−1.6
USA	3,231	3,011	3,025	3,257	3,503	2.0
Belgium	1,454	1,664	1,604	1,740	1,637	3.0
Czech Republic	390	346	350	311	431	2.6
France	8,932	8,781	8,755	8,784	8,849	−0.2
Germany	2,234	2,307	2,385	2,323	2,592	3.8
Greece	1,935	1,824	1,804	1,933	2,314	4.6
Hungary	285	299	325	370	503	15.3
Republic of Ireland	3,372	2,827	2,793	3,095	3,504	1.0
Italy	2,334	2,630	2,790	2,948	3,533	10.9
Netherlands	1,868	1,900	1,943	2,111	2,548	8.1
Poland	1,446	1,573	1,640	1,693	2,033	8.9
Spain	10,654	11,110	11,622	12,246	12,988	5.1
Sweden	369	338	286	283	373	0.3
Egypt	516	407	394	296	298	−12.8
Morocco	305	356	452	460	558	16.3
South Africa	329	343	292	302	343	1.0
Israel	103	88	89	101	102	−0.2
United Arab Emirates	554	580	623	727	786	9.1
India	914	794	837	884	931	0.5
Pakistan	362	416	391	390	417	3.6
Sri Lanka	103	110	99	109	119	3.6
Australia	406	373	409	430	446	2.4
New Zealand	121	108	104	105	118	−0.8

(Continued)

Table 8.2   (Continued)

| | Visits (thousands) | | | | | Average annual growth 2011–15 |
	2011	2012	2013	2014	2015	(%)
Jamaica	221	184	138	220	219	−0.2
Brazil	89	117	97	109	120	7.7
Mexico	299	299	451	434	529	15.4
Total World	56,836	56,538	57,792	60,082	65,720	3.7

Office for National Statistics (2016c)

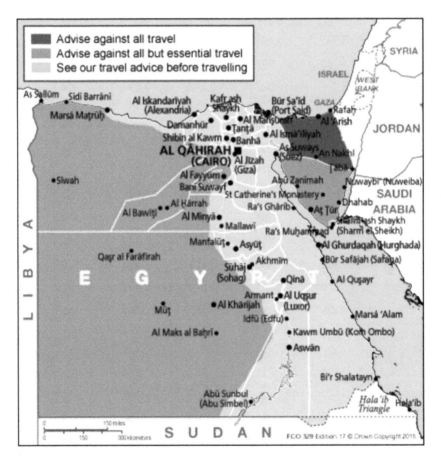

Figure 8.3   'Foreign travel advice: Egypt'

Foreign and Commonwealth Office (released 29 May, 2016)

Figure 8.4   FIFA World Cup Brazil Icon

FIFA Brazil Archive (2014)

It is also worth mentioning that data may appear to tell a different story depending on the form they come in. For instance, compare Table 8.3 and Figure 8.5. Which is 'easier' to understand? Which tells the clearer, or fuller, story?

You will notice that each graphic includes a description, explaining what the map, diagram or numerical data purports to tell you. It is crucial to include a clear description (a bit like a by-line or sub-title) that explains the content of your map, graph, etc. In addition, you may also need to include a 'key' or 'legend'. This explains what the different shading, colours or shapes are intended to represent. Without a description and key, such data are unintelligible.

Table 8.3   Visits to the UK by overseas residents (in thousands), 2006–2015

	North America	Europe	*of which EU*	Other countries	Total world	Percent change
Annual						
2006	4,764	23,377	*21,287*	4,572	32,713	*2.2*
2007	4,403	23,887	*21,824*	4,488	32,778	*0.2*
2008	3,806	23,666	*21,627*	4,416	31,888	*−2.7*
2009	3,564	22,083	*20,331*	4,242	29,889	*−6.3*
2010	3,397	22,046	*20,266*	4,360	29,803	*−0.3*
2011	3,586	22,438	*20,348*	4,774	30,798	*3.3*

(Continued)

Table 8.3   (Continued)

	North America	Europe	of which EU	Other countries	Total world	Percent change
2012	3,544	22,796	20,553	4,744	31,084	0.9
2013	3,509	23,866	21,596	5,318	32,692	5.2
2014	3,625	25,442	23,009	5,310	34,377	5.2
2015	3,974	26,482	24,213	5,659	36,115	5.1

Office for National Statistics (2016d)

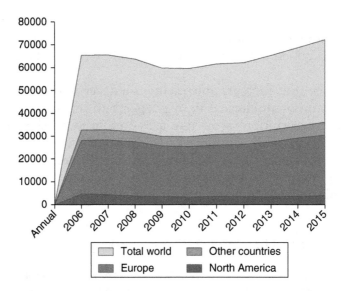

Figure 8.5   Visits to the UK by overseas residents, 2006–2015, omitting detail 'of which EU' (in thousands) (abridged)

Office for National Statistics (2016d)

Finally, if you reproduce or copy sections or selections from maps, diagrams or numerical data as we have here, you will need to give your sources for them. Within the body of the essay, it is often sufficient to refer to these, for example, by saying 'As the data used by Smith show ... (Smith, 2015, p. 15, Table 1)', and providing a full reference at the end of your essay (references are dealt with in detail in Chapter 10).

Using theory, being 'critical'

Essay questions will often require you to explore theoretical arguments as well as concrete examples, and you will also want to draw on other people's theories as evidence to support your own argument. The ability to demonstrate an understanding of competing theoretical positions and to identify the fundamental strengths and weaknesses of each is a basic requirement of undergraduate essay writing. As you develop intermediate and advanced essay-writing skills you will be expected to demonstrate the ability to understand and apply arguments from primary theoretical texts (as opposed to relying on commentaries on these), show an understanding of more complex theoretical positions, be more confident in expressing a reasoned preference for one theoretical position over another, and demonstrate the ability to write from 'within' a perspective or theory.

In working with theories remember that this is like looking through different pairs of spectacles or lenses – they make us see the world in different ways, such as in a poststructuralist or neo-Marxist way. As a result, we have to accept that theories do not let us see the world 'as it is', we see only what they allow us to see. In fact, as we noted in section 2.2, many social scientists argue that we can never see the world 'as it is' and that we always have to look at it from one perspective or another. The task is to find a lens that allows us to view the object under study in as useful a way as possible. These points have some important implications:

- Competing theories are not all equal. Different theories appeal to different kinds of evidence. Different theories are 'useful' in different contexts.
- You cannot lump together the good bits of a whole range of theories to make one 'super-theory'. Different theories will contradict each other. As a result, incorporating an insight from one theory into an existing approach will often require a radical restructuring of both.
- Even when you can make a new theory from aspects of previous ones, you still won't have a view of the world 'as it really is'. You may have a more powerful lens to look through but you will still have to ask yourself the following questions: Is there something beyond the range of this lens that I can't see? Is this lens obscuring what I can see? If I turn to look at a new object, does this lens work equally well?
- Asking these sorts of questions is called being 'critical'. This doesn't mean being negative about everything. It means gaining perspective and being able to see the limitations as well as the strengths of a theory.

Turn to Essays 1 and 2 in Chapter 14. Essay 1 provides a formal example of an essay that demonstrates a systematic engagement with and evaluation of theoretical material. You may want to look, in particular, at the conclusion, where the author attempts to identify some of the limitations of the theoretical arguments in the literature on sex/gender and schooling. You may also want to compare the use of theoretical material in Essay 1 with that in Essay 2. In what ways is Essay 1 more effective in handling and applying theory? You may now wish also to read the tutor comments following each essay.

Writing from 'within' a theory or perspective

At several points in the previous chapters the importance of writing from 'within' a theory or perspective has been highlighted, particularly in the context of more advanced courses. This refers to the ability to take on the conceptual world-view of a particular theoretical standpoint. Individual social scientists are generally identified as working within and contributing to particular theoretical traditions. For example, the work of Professor Stuart Hall is closely identified with a culturalist and poststructuralist re-reading of the Italian Marxist, Antonio Gramsci. The work of Professor Margaret Wetherell is closely identified with a discursive approach to psychology. Like other social scientists, both Hall and Wetherell can be said to write from 'within' the conceptual universe of these specific perspectives. Their work is steeped in the histories of these perspectives; it reproduces and clarifies the perspectives' distinctive vocabularies and conceptual tools, and contributes to knowledge through applying these tools to new objects of enquiry, and by questioning and pushing at the boundaries of their respective traditions.

The ability to write from within a perspective or theory can, then, be said to have at least two important aspects. First, it is a sign of increasing intellectual maturity. It demonstrates a familiarity with, and confidence in handling, the vocabulary and conceptual framework of a particular theoretical tradition. Second, it shows the confidence to take sides in intellectual debates. As a social scientist your duty to evaluate critically does not mean that you should adopt a uniform and bland relativism where all forms of knowledge are considered equally useful. The point of writing from 'within' a particular perspective or theory is that you are prepared to take a stand and say, 'This is useful knowledge'. This does not mean that you should attempt to shape evidence to fit a preconceived standpoint. It means taking an informed position on the basis of reasoned academic judgement and with due reference to the potential limits of your own arguments. An example of a student essay in which the author clearly writes from 'within' a perspective (social constructionism) and uses this to take up a firm position on the set question can be found in Essay 1 in Chapter 14.

However, it is worth stressing that essay questions will not necessarily require that you write from 'within' a perspective or theory. Indeed, they may specify that you should adopt an explicitly neutral position, standing 'outside' one or more positions in order to evaluate them critically.

Importantly, keep in mind that it will not always be possible to make a reasoned judgement between competing positions. After careful consideration, you may decide that the explanations they offer are equally strong or equally weak. If this is the case, you should say so.

Being 'self-reflexive'

In the social sciences, choosing between competing theories or arguments will, at some point, involve making a value judgement. Although it may be possible to identify clear reasons why some arguments are more persuasive than others, our choice will almost inevitably be shaped by our political, moral and philosophical values. While not all social scientific writing will demonstrate this, it is good practice to make explicit the theoretical or political orientation that underpins your work rather than pretending that your argument is simply 'objective'. For example, you might indicate that the essay is being written from 'within' a feminist, or Foucauldian, or cognitive development perspective. This will alert readers to possible bias or areas of partiality in your argument, and will allow them to make up their own minds about the strengths of your case. In fact, by signalling your possible blindspots to the reader, you are being more objective than if you pretended such blindspots did not exist.

The idea of being self-reflexive relates to two other important points raised in this book. The first is the use of the first person pronoun, 'I'. This is covered in more detail in section 12.2, which you may wish to turn to now; briefly, however, there are some social science essays where using 'I' is not only acceptable, but is in accord with the subject and approach taken. The second point relates to this. In section 11.3 we consider the *reflective* essay as it relates to a more conventional social science essay. The reflective essay *expects* the author's subjectivity to inform their thinking and writing, and indeed the author, her or his experiences, responses and reflections, may be central to the essay. Particularly if you are on an applied or practical course, you may frequently be asked to engage in such reflection. Being self-reflexive takes reflection to a deeper level, encouraging the author to consider their alignment with different theories or theorists, and what issues – including, for instance, the 'differences that make a difference' – may inflect their interests.

Summary

- As you progress to more advanced undergraduate courses you will increasingly be required to select relevant material from a range of sources and relate this back to the individual essay question.
- Arguments should be supported with appropriate illustrations and evidence. Try to select a range of the most significant examples – some will be richer and more far-reaching than others. Examples should relate back to the essay question and support the argument you are making.
- For some courses you will need to use maps, diagrams or numerical data. These can help support your argument, but remember that they are not 'hard facts' and are subject to interpretation.
- Social science essays will often ask you to explore theoretical arguments and use these as evidence as well as concrete examples. As you develop your essay-writing skills you will need to show increasing confidence in exploring the strengths and weaknesses of competing theories.
- Some theories are stronger and more convincing than others; theories cannot necessarily be lumped together to make a 'super-theory' – they often contradict each other. In handling theories, social scientists need to be 'critical', that is, they need to display an awareness of a theory's weaknesses and its strengths. However, one sign of increasing intellectual maturity is the ability to write from 'within' a perspective.
- Being 'self-reflexive' means acknowledging your own particular biases, for example, by indicating that you are arguing from a specific point of view. Reflecting on experiences, ideas and your own background may be part of engaging in self-reflexivity.

8.3 Adding weight to your argument

Social scientists highlight key works and use quotations for the following reasons:

- As a source of evidence, that is, to support and illustrate their own points
- To provide the reader with a 'map' of the most important work done in the area under discussion
- To demonstrate to the reader that they have thought about and understood what other people have written on a subject, and that their own arguments should be taken seriously.

As you progress to intermediate and more advanced undergraduate courses, you should expect to demonstrate an increased ability to select appropriate quotations and cite key texts in order to add weight to your argument.

Let's take a brief look at some examples of these strategies in operation. In Paško Bilić's article on the social construction of knowledge on English Wikipedia, he begins by setting out his intellectual stall, citing some of the significant theorists in the fields of media, communication and the network society (Bauman, Berger and Luckmann, Castells, etc.). In the following section he narrows his focus and, at the same time, gives an implicit explanation for why he thinks English Wikipedia is worthy of study, using two direct quotes – one longer (over 30 words), one very short – to support his points:

> Luhmann (1986) argues that communication is essential to sustaining and maintaining social systems. ... However, while face-to-face communication is essential as a foundation of society and social systems, different technologies alter the communication types and communicative possibilities of human beings. Altheide and Snow (Altheide and Snow, 1979: 16) argue that through adopting a media logic people have
>
> > developed a consciousness that affects how they perceive, define, and deal with their environment. What emerges as knowledge in contemporary society is, to a significant extent, the result of this media consciousness.
>
> In a very general sense, the medium is 'something that modifies communication' on four different levels: as a technology, as a societal institution, as an organizational machine and way of setting content in a scene, and as a space of experience for a recipient (Krotz, 2009: 23).
>
> (Bilić, 2015, p. 1261)

Bilić is situating wikis in a longer-term academic discussion about communication and (media) technology. The quotes add weight and clarity to the section, and pull together two key points – that consciousness and communication are both altered with the adoption of new media.

In the following, Bilić explores Wikipedia's role in constructing social knowledge:

> Through technological preconditions and continued communication and interaction between the editors, wikis and wiki-based projects serve as 'knowledge-building environments'. This term is used in educational psychology to emphasize the role of technologies for supporting constructive, collective and open knowledge-building processes (Scardamalia and Bereiter, 1994). Forte and Bruckman (2007) analysed wikis as potentially powerful learning tools in educational contexts for collaborative construction of texts. Kimmerle et al. (2010, 2011) used Wikipedia as an example of 'knowledge-building' and emphasized how collaboration leads to 'co-evolution' of the individual knowledge of contributors and collective knowledge shared within the community of collaborators. Halatchliyski et al.

(2010) also argued that wikis are 'knowledge-building environments' that consist of three dimensions: a content dimension, or the current status of knowledge in the community; discursive dimension or the process of how the knowledge was constructed; and network dimension or the structure of the community with the relative position of its authors.

(Bilić, 2015, p. 1263)

In this paragraph, Bilić indicates the depth of the research on which he is drawing, citing authors from the fields of educational psychology, educational technology and sociology. He also enriches the broad phrase 'knowledge-building environments' as it describes wikis, citing Halatchliyski et al., who say there are three dimensions to this knowledge-building. Bilić adds authority to his claim by citing the names of the authors on whom he draws, using the language of the field, in particular 'knowledge-building' and 'co-evolution' which are in quotation marks, and by succinctly paraphrasing (and adding a bit of explanation of) the 'three dimensions'. From a reader's perspective, this is a lovely, clear paragraph that:

- sets out Bilić's claim at the start: ' … wikis … serve as "knowledge-building environments"';
- lends weight to his claim by citing authors from different (though related) fields, and by inserting quotes to show he is using 'their' language;
- develops the complexity of what is meant by knowledge-building by paraphrasing Halatchliyski et al.

There are several points that are worth pulling out of these examples:

- In each case, the writer uses his quotations or citations of other authors to support a point that he himself is making. This is important because there is a temptation to let longer quotations in particular do the work for you. Quotations and references to other people's work should support rather than replace your argument.
- In the case of the direct quotations, Bilić has chosen these because they succinctly express a point, thereby allowing him adroitly to link two ideas.
- Bilić tells us clearly who is speaking, either by introducing the author at the beginning of a sentence, e.g. 'Altheide and Snow (Altheide and Snow, 1979: 16) argue that …', or by making the claim/introducing the quote himself but attributing it at the end, e.g. 'the medium is "something that modifies communication" on four different levels … (Krotz, 2009: 23)'. Quotations or claims that are not introduced in some way can sometimes read as if they have appeared out of nowhere and interrupt the 'flow' of the writing.
- The first (longer) quotation is indented. It is usual to indent longer quotations (over 30 words) on the left margin – and sometimes on the right as well – to distinguish them from your own argument. Indented quotations do not have inverted commas – or quotation marks – around them. The second, shorter quotation is enclosed in quotation marks, and falls within the line of the sentence.

- Shortening or adding to your quoted material needs to be shown. If you leave out phrases or sentences, indicate such cuts with three dots (…), known as an ellipsis, as we have done following Bilić's first sentence. Similarly, if you need to add or substitute a word, letter or phrase to clarify the sense, put your inserted words in square brackets. For instance, we might want to say: '[W]ikis and wiki-based projects serve as "knowledge-building environments"', according to Paško Bilić. The words quoted here originally appear mid-sentence, and the 'w' in 'wiki' is lower-case; as the phrase now begins a sentence, our inserted 'W' is capitalized and in brackets.
- Bilić is very careful to provide references for the work cited. He has used a referencing system similar to Harvard (this is explained in detail in Chapter 10), providing in-text short citations, which are followed up with full-length citations in his reference list at the end.

Summary

- As your skills develop, and certainly at intermediate and advanced standards, you should be able to select appropriate quotations and cite key texts in support of your argument.
- Quotations and references to key texts are used: as a source of evidence; to provide the reader with a 'map' of the most important works in an area; and to give the work 'authority'.
- Quotations should be introduced.
- Shorter quotations can be written in the main text in single inverted commas. Longer quotations should be written in a separate paragraph indented at the left-hand (and sometimes right-hand) margins. Any alterations to the original quotation should be indicated.
- Quotations and key texts highlighted in an essay must be supported by a reference, in the style preferred by your tutor or university.

8.4 Communicating your argument

You may feel happy that you have grasped the essay question and are able to answer it comprehensively and logically, but to prove this you will need to be able to convey your ideas clearly to your reader.

Thinking about the audience

Students often ask who their reader is meant to be. Commonly, this reader is identified as the 'intelligent layperson'. While this notion is useful, it presents problems in that even the intelligent layperson cannot be expected to know much of the technical vocabulary that is taken for granted in the social sciences. Perhaps a more useful idea is to think of your reader as someone studying the social sciences at the same level as you but at another university. You can assume that your reader will have a grasp of basic social scientific ideas, so you won't need to explain every last detail to them. However, they won't necessarily be studying the same things as you, so you will need to explain more complex ideas and be careful to define your terms. For the most advanced university courses you can assume that your reader will have a greater degree of sophistication and you can therefore afford to write with more complexity. In fact, by the end of advanced university courses you should probably aim to be writing for an expert audience.

Clear sentences and paragraphs

Sentences are the building blocks of paragraphs, which in turn are the building blocks of arguments – and essays. The general rule in essay writing is to keep your sentences simple and easily understood. However, like other academic fields, the social sciences tend to have formal written styles and specialized vocabularies. Social scientific vocabulary cannot be dismissed simply as 'jargon' (although sometimes this might be a justified criticism). Academic disciplines need complex lexicons to be able to deal with complex issues.

Unfortunately, this may cause you problems. There is a real danger that in trying to sound 'academic' you may simply sound confused. The best advice is probably to say that, if you are unsure, use the language that you understand. Even when you feel more confident you need to remember that there is nothing to be gained from using complex terminology for its own sake. The real test lies in being able to communicate complex ideas in the form that is most easily understood.

Here's an example of a sentence from a cultural geography essay on territories and flows that usefully mixes academic and everyday language.

> Although imperial bioprospecting has taken place historically, more recently, the pace and scale of transforming plants and their component parts into commercially viable drugs has gathered speed.

'Bioprospecting' may be an unfamiliar term, but it is cleverly explained within the sentence as 'transforming plants and their component parts into commercially viable drugs'. This clause (or section of the sentence) is written in everyday language. More clever still is the other work this sentence does. The author indicates that bioprospecting is not new – it is part of an imperialist legacy – but its acceleration and increased scope *are* new. Again, this is straightforward language that sets out the author's stall for the rest of the paragraph.

The paragraph proceeds to give information about how international agreements have sought both to regulate and deregulate bioprospecting. The author uses this evidence to lead to the paragraph's final sentence:

This form of territory and flow ... continues to be contentious as it is the industrialised north that continues to benefit economically from the rich biodiversity and historical knowledge of the south (Bingham, 2008).

This sentence uses terminology from the set essay question, 'territory and flow', says that bioprospecting is contentious, and then boldly states why: it is the north that benefits from the south's biodiversity/knowledge. This is a complex statement, but as the student understands the terminology she is using and has expressed this clearly, even non-specialists will get the gist.

A common trick to help you express an idea in a sentence is, simply, to say it out loud. If the sentence sounds odd to you, break it down into its component parts: is there a particular word that feels uncomfortable? Look it up in your dictionary (if you haven't done so already, you would be wise to invest in a specialist dictionary for your subject area). If we wanted to simplify the first sentence, we might break it down like this:

Bioprospecting – extracting plants or their component parts for the purposes of making money – has a long history. While this history can be traced back to the period of British imperialism, in recent years the pace and scale of bioprospecting have accelerated.

This is less elegant than the original, but it still does most of the job, although you will notice that despite using more words the point about turning plants into commercially lucrative drugs is missing.

As with sentences, your paragraphs need to be as clear as possible. The 'Rubin method' of paragraph analysis (Rubin, 1983) suggests that paragraphs have:

- a topic;
- a series of statements that explain what the author thinks is special or relevant about the topic;

and that, put together, these form the paragraph's

- main idea.

Each paragraph should address one key point or one aspect of a key point. Look again at the Bilić examples in section 8.3. Does using the Rubin method help you discern the 'main idea' in each?

Giving the essay direction

If readers are to avoid getting lost in your argument you need to tell them what is happening at key points along the way. There are three effective ways to do this:

- introduce and summarize the main sections;
- recap and signpost your argument;
- where useful, remind the reader of the subject of your essay.

These points are elaborated below but you can also see them applied in Essays 1 and 3 in Chapter 14.

Introducing and summarizing the main sections

To illustrate this point, here is an example from a chapter in which the author, Geoff Andrews, explores the history of political dissent in the UK, and the ways in which dissent works as a set of 'living ideas':

> The discussion in the previous section focused on the ways in which ideas of dissent were articulated in a particular historical context and some of the impacts that they had – both for the lives of the dissidents, but also crucially for ... political rulers. ... Therefore, from this example, we can say that dissent was a type of political participation which questioned the 'legitimacy' of the political system, its institutions, laws and policies, but also its dominant values. ...
>
> It is important to recognize how, in this case, dissent worked as a set of living ideas. The writings of intellectuals, the language of a popular pamphlet, the force of sermons and the discussions in the coffee houses helped produce a critique of the way politics was conducted and power was distributed. In this respect the impact of dissent as a set of living ideas is clear. ...
>
> However, there is a second way in which dissent worked as a set of living ideas at this time. The ideas of thinkers such as Godwin, Paine and Wollstonecraft were also to become part of a wider chain of ideas that developed into political ideologies. ...
>
> (Andrews, 2005, pp. 82–3)

If we break down this passage we can see Andrews does the following:

- He first reiterates the key point from his previous section ('the ways in which ideas of dissent were articulated in a particular historical context and some of the impacts that they had'), thus underscoring the argument of this particular section.
- Next, he reminds the reader of one of the overarching ideas running through his argument as a whole ('It is important to recognize how, in this case, dissent worked as a set of living ideas'). This creates a 'bridge' between his previous point and the one he is about to make.
- He then introduces his new point ('However, there is a second way in which dissent worked as a set of living ideas at this time') before signposting the focus of this (dissenting thought 'developed into political ideologies').

Recapping and signposting

Throughout his chapter, Andrews carefully recaps and signposts his argument as a means of binding the argument together. One frequently used device for signposting in academic writing is to indicate that there are various issues you aim to explore and then to list these as you discuss them. For instance, later in his discussion of political dissent, Andrews writes:

> The remainder of this section will expand on these three liberal justifications for the rights of dissidents. ... First, the liberal emphasis on liberty as the core principle was on the basis that liberals should be left to their own choices. They know their own interests best, and it is not the business of the state (or any other 'collective body') to interfere with freedom of thought or expression. ...
>
> This view introduces the second liberal defence of dissent, which is that it was essential to progress. This position was apparent in Godwin's belief that the spirit of free enquiry would ultimately win out over ignorance and would be reflected in increasingly harmonious ways of living. ...
>
> Third, liberals have justified dissent on democratic-pluralist grounds. In modern liberal democratic societies, where individuals are equal before the law ... dissent is an essential part of the political process.
>
> (Andrews, 2005, pp. 87–8)

Although there isn't the space to include the full details of Andrews' argument, you can see from the above extract how he first signposts ('The remainder of this section will expand on these three liberal justifications ...') and then identifies the three points being made ('This view introduces the second liberal defence of dissent'). This strategy is an important means by which he helps us as readers locate ourselves within his ongoing discussion.

Having carefully developed his argument in this section of the chapter, Andrews then brings it to a close by recapping its core points. Because the chapter was written as a teaching text, Andrews does this in the form of a bullet-pointed list. This would be unusual in a formal social sciences essay where the expectation would usually be for arguments to be made using conventional paragraphs (though see section 11.2 on report-writing). If his summary had been written in the conventional essay form it might have looked something like this:

> As the above points suggest, dissent occupies an important position in liberal theory. For liberal theory, dissent provides the opportunity for free expression, pluralism and progress.
>
> (Adapted from Andrews, 2005, p. 90)

As with his use of signposting, the careful manner in which Andrews recaps the major points in his argument underlines these and helps the reader to orient her- or himself within it.

Referring back to the subject or task of the essay

Referring back to the subject or task of the essay involves reminding the reader of your main topic, arguments or themes, or the task you are undertaking. This is another way in which writers help to focus readers' attention and thus orient them within the argument. An obvious way to do this is, at strategic moments, to repeat the essay title. However, this can be clumsy or repetitious. You don't want your essay overburdened with phrases such as, 'In answering the question, "Evaluate the importance of the unconscious in Freud's theory of the mind" it is thus necessary to … '. This is why referring back to the subject or task of the essay is perhaps best achieved by having a strong sense of these in your own mind. For instance, in one of the extracts explored above, we noted that Andrews drew attention to an over-arching point in his argument (dissent as a 'living idea') when making a 'bridge' between one section and the next. In other words, Andrews' task in this section of his chapter was to convey the notion of dissent as a living idea and, in summarizing this section and introducing the next one, he carefully related the argument back to this task ('It is important to recognize how, in this case, dissent worked as a set of living ideas … ').

Making your essay 'flow'

Link or 'transition' words, phrases and sentences are used to make an essay 'flow'; that is, they make the writing easy to read by relating sentences, parts of sentences and paragraphs to each other. We can illustrate this by taking a final look at an extract from Andrews' chapter on political dissent:

> A further question worth posing here is whether dissent can take violent forms. Is terrorism a form of dissent, for example? There is no easy answer to this. Many political theorists and writers would add the qualification of 'legitimate' or 'illegitimate' dissent. That is, dissent expressed in liberal democratic societies is only legitimate if it does not resort to violence. Yet this seems to take us only part of the way. For example, deciding what is legitimate or illegitimate dissent will depend to some extent on ideological assumptions, cultural influences and political tradition. Meanings can also change over time, suggesting that one person's freedom fighter is another person's terrorist. This was the case with the African National Congress (ANC) for example, described by many opponents (including the

Thatcher governments in the UK in the 1980s) as 'terrorist' because of its commitment to armed struggle. Yet following the release of Nelson Mandela in 1989 and the participation in the new post-apartheid South African government in the 1990s, this description was changed and the ANC became regarded as a mainstream political organization.

(Andrews, 2005, p. 74)

Now re-read the extract with many of the link words and phrases removed:

A further question worth posing here is whether dissent can take violent forms. Is terrorism a form of dissent? There is no easy answer. Many political theorists and writers would add the qualification of 'legitimate' or 'illegitimate' dissent. Dissent expressed in liberal democratic societies is only legitimate if it does not resort to violence. This seems to take us only part of the way. Deciding what is legitimate or illegitimate dissent will depend to some extent on ideological assumptions, cultural influences and political tradition. Meanings can change over time, suggesting that one person's freedom fighter is another person's terrorist. The African National Congress (ANC) was described by many opponents (including the Thatcher governments in the UK in the 1980s) as 'terrorist' because of its commitment to armed struggle. Following the release of Nelson Mandela in 1989 and the participation in the new post-apartheid South African government in the 1990s, this description was changed. The ANC became regarded as a mainstream political organization.

(Adapted from Andrews, 2005, p. 74)

Although some of the phrasing in this revised paragraph might seem punchier, much of the extract now reads like a list of unrelated points or something written in note form. In consequence, the reader is jolted from one sentence to another. In making sure you link sentences, parts of sentences and paragraphs, you ensure that your reader's attention remains focused on the argument and does not become distracted by your writing.

Summary

- One way to think of your notional reader is as someone studying the social sciences at an equivalent level in another university. She or he will understand basic social scientific concepts but won't necessarily be familiar with the area addressed in your essay. By the end of advanced undergraduate courses you should aim to write for an 'expert' audience.

(Continued)

(Continued)

- The aim of good essay writing is to convey complex ideas in as clear a form as possible.
- Sentences should work as the building blocks of paragraphs. If a sentence, or phrase within a sentence, isn't clear to you, break it down into smaller parts until it is.
- Paragraphs contain a topic and a series of statements explaining what is relevant about this topic. Together these make up its 'main idea'.
- You can give your essay a strong sense of direction by: introducing and summarizing main sections; recapping and signposting your argument; and, where useful, referring back to the question.
- Using link words and sentences ensures that your essay flows smoothly.

Self-test

1 What are the three main stages in setting out an argument?
2 What does it mean to work 'from the general to the particular'?
3 What does it mean to write from 'within a theory or perspective'?
4 How do social scientists add 'authority' to their claims?
5 What is the Rubin method?
6 There are three main ways to give your essay direction. What are they?
7 What is the role of link or transition words and phrases?

Don't forget! Visit **https://study.sagepub.com/redmanandmaples5** for more tasks and resources related to this chapter.

9

Writing Conclusions

- What a conclusion should aim to do – and should not do
- What a conclusion should contain

Conclusions are an important part of an essay, and a well-written conclusion is a good way of picking up extra marks.

9.1 What a conclusion should aim to do – and should not do

The primary job of a conclusion is to provide a final condensed version of the essay's core argument, and in the process to provide an overview of the state of 'current knowledge' or 'current opinion' on the given topic. Since your conclusion should take up no more than 10 per cent of your essay, a short essay (of up to 1,500 words) won't have room to do much more than this. However, if you are writing a longer essay your conclusion should do the following:

- Recap the key points in your argument/summarize the key debates raised by the question, and try to synthesize them;
- Provide a final condensed version of the essay's core argument that restates your position on the question;
- If necessary, identify absences in your argument that could be explored in future work.

Put simply, a conclusion should leave the reader with a clear impression of your argument – what it was about, what you believe, and why you believe this. An introductory-level essay is likely to demonstrate the ability to summarize content clearly and concisely. More advanced essays will be expected to progress towards writing more complex conclusions that emphasize condensed versions of your core argument.

One thing that a conclusion should not do is bring in any new material or new ideas or arguments. Some students have a tendency to 'tack on' points that they forgot to mention or didn't have space for in the main part of their essay. However, effectively saying 'And another thing!' will not gain you marks and may suggest to your tutor that your essay wasn't as well planned, or your ideas as well developed, as they might have been.

9.2 What a conclusion should contain

If you have read the chapter on writing introductions, you will remember the following question and introduction:

> 'Evaluate the claim that *Coronation Street* is the most enjoyable contemporary British soap opera.'

> *Coronation Street* consistently receives high viewer ratings. This essay explores the basis of this popularity, evaluating its appeal in comparison with *EastEnders*, one of its major ratings rivals. In its opening section, the essay uses a feminist analysis to argue that *Coronation Street*'s appeal may be found in its 'women-centredness', in particular its focus on strong female characters, its exploration of women's lives, and its often humorous treatment of men. The essay then goes on to explore the contrasting approach adopted in *EastEnders*, which has often focused on social issues and emphasized a 'gritty realism'. The essay argues that, in comparison to *Coronation Street*, this 'gritty realism' fails to connect with women's culture and that it is the appeal to women of these less naturalistic elements that underlies *Coronation Street*'s continuing popularity.

Imagine that we now have to write a conclusion to the same essay. We will have written a main section that develops these arguments and provides supporting evidence to back up and illustrate our claims. We now have to bring the essay to a close, leaving the reader with a clear overall impression of our argument and our reasons for holding this position. From the introduction it's clear that the main thrust of our argument is that *Coronation Street*'s appeal lies in the way it speaks to women about their experiences and women's culture. As a result, we may well write a conclusion that looks something like the following:

> This essay has argued that, historically, *EastEnders* has adopted broadly 'realist' genre conventions. It has, for example, emphasized social

diversity (witness the presence of gay characters and characters from black and minority ethnic groups). Similarly, it has sought to address 'difficult' social issues such as HIV infection and unemployment. In contrast, despite covering some of the same territory, *Coronation Street* has tended to adopt a more diluted naturalism. In particular, in preference to *EastEnders*' 'gritty realism', it has tended to emphasize strong female characters and has portrayed a rich array of comic situations, events and individuals, frequently at the expense of men. As the essay has suggested, it is possible to argue that these aspects of *Coronation Street* connect with the everyday cultures of its female audience and that the programme's women-centredness is central to its continuing strong position in the television ratings war.

If we break down this conclusion into its component parts, we can see that it does the following:

- Recaps the key stages in the argument and summarizes the key debates raised by the question (that is, the argument that *EastEnders* favours 'gritty realism' while *Coronation Street* is less naturalistic but more women-centred);
- Provides a final condensed statement of the essay's core argument (this women-centredness underlies its popular appeal).

This conclusion hasn't identified absences in the argument that could be explored in future work, and it isn't always necessary to do this. However, what if in the main section of the essay we had provided examples illustrating *Coronation Street*'s putative 'woman-centredness', but had not established (via audience research) that this was what actually appealed to women viewers? In this case, our conclusion might suggest that further research was necessary to substantiate (or falsify) our hypothesis. This, then, is an absence in our argument that could be explored in future work.

The above is one conclusion that we might have written to this particular essay question. However, you might disagree with the argument and want to write something completely different. Equally, you could have expressed the same points in a number of different ways. Alternatively, you may feel that you couldn't write a conclusion like this because it is 'too complicated' or 'too well written'. If this is the case, don't worry. You could write a serviceable conclusion in a much simpler form. The point is that there is more than one way to write a conclusion, and you should not view this example as a template to be followed slavishly.

If you want to look at more formal examples of social science essay conclusions, you should read Essays 1 and 3 in Chapter 14. In both cases the author summarizes the argument, while also taking a clear stand in relation to the question. Essay 1 also indicates some possible limitations in the literature. Compare this to the conclusions of Essays 2 and 4. Why are the conclusions to Essays 1 and 3 more successful?

Summary

- The primary job of a conclusion is to provide a final condensed version of your essay's core argument and thereby to summarize the key debates raised by the question, or provide an overview of 'current knowledge', as presented by you, on your given topic.
- The conclusion should not contain any new material.
- The conclusion should take up roughly 10 per cent of an essay.
- Shorter conclusions should provide a condensed version of the essay's core topics, and demonstrate that the essay has addressed the key debates/issues/evidence raised by the question.
- Longer conclusions should: recap the subject of the essay in some form; recap the key stages in the argument/summarize the key debates raised by the question; provide a final condensed version of the argument that restates the essay's position on the question; (if necessary) identify absences in the argument that could be explored in future work.
- An essay written to an 'introductory' standard might be expected to provide a conclusion that demonstrates an ability to summarize the content of the essay clearly and concisely. More advanced essays should move towards conclusions that emphasize sophisticated condensed versions of the core argument, and a sophisticated understanding of the key debates raised by the question.

Self-test

1 What is the purpose of a conclusion?
2 What should a conclusion *not* contain?
3 What might distinguish a conclusion written to an introductory standard from one written to an advanced standard?

Don't forget! Visit **https://study.sagepub.com/redmanandmaples5** for more tasks and resources related to this chapter.

10

Referencing

- What is a reference?
- Why are references needed?
- What should be referenced?
- Basic principles
- Advanced referencing
- Compiling your references

10.1 What is a reference?

In short, references are an acknowledgement of other people's work. They are a way of indicating, according to accepted convention, that you have drawn upon, been inspired by, wish to argue against, someone else; and not just anyone, but a particular person, group of people or institution. References name that person or group. References indicate that you are familiar with a 'body of work'. They demonstrate that you have taken the trouble to discover who has said what in your field before you.

There are a number of terms that are used to describe different aspects of referencing, and they are not always used consistently. However, it may help to review the following terms: 'reference', 'citation', 'source' and 'bibliography'.

'Reference' is often used as a generic term. Broadly speaking, this is when you identify or 'refer to' someone else, or more particularly their work. Your list of references at the end of an essay will contain a series of 'citations'. Citations are more specifically the notes on where to find the material you have cited: Redman, P. and Maples, W. (2017) *Good Essay Writing: A Social Sciences Guide*, 5th edn., London, Sage. However, 'citation' and 'reference' are often used interchangeably. 'Source' is a bit more distinctive. Sources may be individuals you have interviewed, local government archives, a website, or a particular journal or key author. When you are writing your essay, you need to cite your sources, and provide a list of references for them at the end. In some disciplines and in different countries, you may instead be asked for a bibliography at the end of your work. Again, there is a bit of an overlap in the common use of 'reference list' and 'bibliography', but broadly speaking reference lists are appropriate for shorter, undergraduate essays, where all material that is used to inform the essay will have been directly cited within the text. Bibliographies could well include books and articles, websites, films, etc., that have been employed (for example as 'background' reading) during research, but may not have been directly referenced in the final written work. You will more commonly find bibliographies at the end of dissertations, textbooks or monographs.

Reference writing may seem like a banal clerical activity, and it usually takes much longer than you could possibly imagine. So why do you have to do it?

10.2 Why are references needed?

There are several reasons why proper referencing is important. First, as noted above, it acknowledges your sources and demonstrates that you are familiar with the key material on your topic and are knowledgeable about it. Second, it guards against plagiarism, or accusations of plagiarism, since good referencing clearly shows the source of any data or arguments you use that are not your own. Third, good referencing allows the person who is reading your assignment to follow up any work you mention that sounds particularly interesting, or that he or she does not know. In order to do this the reader needs as much information as possible so he or she can more easily find the work in a library, bookshop or on the internet. Fourth, having a sound referencing system will help you remember particular points, or pieces of work and who said or wrote them. Finally, an essay that is properly referenced looks like a professional piece of writing, worthy of academic respect. Put another way:

- References assert the 'authority' of your argument;
- They allow readers to check the accuracy of the claims that your essay makes;
- References allow your readers to look up a source or argument that they want to know more about;
- They act as a reminder to you of the sources you used, and make it easier for you to follow up or go back to ideas at a later stage;
- They are part of academic convention; presenting proper references shows you understand academic principles.

Related to this final point, references are also common courtesy. As you are part of an academic community, it is only right and courteous that you should acknowledge the work of others in your community.

10.3 What should be referenced?

The following items need to be referenced:

- Quotations;
- Diagrams, statistical information or maps reproduced or cited in your essay;
- Work that is referred to but not quoted directly (for example, if you have written 'Hall (2004) argues that … ' or 'Research by Szerszynski (2010) suggests that … ');
- Otherwise unsubstantiated arguments and assertions (for example, if you have written, 'It is arguable that conventional notions of "normality" have been fundamentally challenged by the disability rights movement' or, 'Several commentators have argued … ', you could then insert a reference or references which indicate to the reader that this idea has a considerable degree of academic respectability – in other words, there are a number of legitimate sources who have made the same or similar suggestions).

10.4 Basic principles

There are many ways to write references, but all have one feature in common: clear, unambiguous information that allows you or your reader to locate the work. You will find online support, such as EasyBib (www.easybib.com), CiteThisForMe (www.citethisforme.com) or North Carolina State University's Citation Builder (www.lib.ncsu.edu/citationbuilder/), invaluable in automating your referencing, but please remember that there are different citation styles – for instance, Citation Builder doesn't use the Harvard style (though the Chicago 'author/date' or American Psychological Association (APA) styles are similar) – and that you need to be consistent in your style of referencing. This chapter demonstrates a version of the Harvard system, commonly used in the social sciences. However, while we find Harvard perhaps the easiest system available, your university may well prefer that you use a different style. You may also find there is one referencing preference in the psychology department and another in sociology. For this reason alone, you would be wise to keep a database of references using software that allows translation between styles. Some universities have their own proprietary systems, but commonly available systems include: RefME (www.refme.com/uk) and Zotero (www.zotero.org).

It is also worth mentioning that as the range of online academic sources increases, referencing styles will adapt: it is only relatively recently that the Harvard system introduced express formatting for online lectures such as those available through TED (www.ted.com) or on YouTube (www.youtube.com). Up-to-date software will help you manage as changes take place.

What follows are common citations, given with the intention of familiarizing you with the principles behind academic referencing formats: as we are concerned with principles, and as this is intended to be a short guide, this section is in no way comprehensive. Again, using referencing software will enable you to check even the most idiosyncratic citation.

Finding the details for references

Referencing software is helpful, as is understanding the principles of referencing, but before you can put together a citation, you need to find the 'ingredients'. The publication details for books are given on the 'imprint' page, which usually comes after the title page. Have a look at *Good Essay Writing*'s imprint page now. You will see a lot of information about copyright, the publisher's addresses, and information about printing. You may have to look carefully to find the referencing information you want, which is: date of publication (of this edition), edition number, location of the publisher, the name of the publisher. You will know the name of the author(s) or editor(s) and the title of the book (and its subtitle) from the title page. Journals – particularly those accessed online – will often have a 'flag' that says 'To reference (or cite) this article', followed by the necessary information. All online sources should include the URL, which, if it isn't listed on the PDF or on-screen text, can be copied and pasted from your browser.

Abbreviated references in the body of the text, including an example for a single author book

Let's consider the basic principles for abbreviated references appearing in the main body of your essay as used for a book with a single author. Having written a quotation you simply add immediately after it an abbreviated reference, for example:

> 'All sections of society live longer in countries that are more egalitarian' (Dorling, 2014, p. 130).

Note that the full stop goes outside the bracket since the abbreviated reference is all part of the sentence. If you want to use the author's name in your sentence, you can also write your reference like this:

Dorling claims that in counties 'that are more egalitarian', such as Japan, '[a]ll sections of society live longer' (2014, p. 130).

Abbreviated references should contain information in the following order:

- Author's last name;
- Date of publication (make sure this is the date of the edition in your hand or on your screen);
- If applicable (for example if using a direct quotation or referring to a specific point), the page number(s).

If your quote is a long one (more than 30 words or two lines), then it should be indented and you should dispose of opening and closing quotation marks. Your abbreviated reference should then fall in the line immediately following the quotation.

Old age is surrounded with perceptions which have been called the myths of old age (Sidell, 1995). Such myths include that older people are a homogenous group; that ill health can be expected in old age (Sidell, 1995, p. xvi); in turn leading to a commonly held belief that older people are a burden, as they experience such ill health and physical decline. The homogenous grouping of older people together has been robustly challenged (Dressel et al., 1997), with differences along class, gender and race divisions now widely accepted to have an impact on an individual's experience of ageing.

(Innis, 2010, pp. 19–20)

All your abbreviated references must be expanded into full references in a list at the end of your essay.

List of full references at the end of the text

At the end of your essay, in a list headed 'References' or 'Reference List', you need to write out all your references in full, organized alphabetically by authors' surnames. Let's consider first the Dorling example above. In the reference list the entry would be:

Dorling, D. (2014) *Inequality and the 1%*, London, Verso.

This entry is typical of those for a book with a single author. All similar entries in the Harvard system should:

- Begin with the author's surname and initial(s);
- Give the date of publication (of the relevant edition);

- Give the title of the work;
- Give the place of publication;
- End with the name of the publisher.

Here is a simple template:

Author's last name, First name initial(s). (date) *Title of the book*, Location of the publisher, Publisher.

For books, you won't need to include individual page numbers in the long reference – however, see below for conventions for journal articles and *chapters* in books. Your list of references will look similar to the one at the end of this book.

Basic conventions

The example we have just looked at is of a single author book, but of course you will find that material quoted or referred to can come from many different types of sources, and your reference list must reflect this. Unfortunately the basic referencing system needs a little more embellishment to cover the extra details for all but the most straightforward citations. More examples of commonly cited sources are given below.

First, though, let's just note a few more basic conventions that are helpful to remember:

- Titles of major works, programmes, etc. (such as book and journal titles) are set in *italics* or underlined;
- Parts of works or minor works (such as articles within journals or chapters within edited collections) are put in 'single quotation marks'.

Sometimes you will need to reference a number of works by the same author that happen to have been published in the same year. How do you differentiate these when giving an abbreviated reference? The solution is to label them '2010a', '2010b' and so on. Thus, you might write, 'Szerszynski (2010a, 2010b) argues that ...'. When giving the full references at the end of the essay, you would then list them with the 2010a entry followed by the 2010b entry. (The order of 'a' and 'b' is usually determined by the order in which the references appear in the essay.) Where you cite work by the same author from more than one year, your reference list will cite the publications in reverse chronological order (the most recent work first).

If in your essay you have more than one text to reference in one citation, list these alphabetically, for example: (Dorling, 2014; Frosh et al., 2002; Haywood and Mac an Ghaill, 2003).

Edition numbers

Books are not only reprinted but can also be revised and republished as new *editions*. It is important to include the edition number of a text in the full reference:

Castells, M. (2015) *Networks of Outrage and Hope: Social Movements in the Internet Age*, 2nd edn., Cambridge, Polity Press.

Online sources

The convention for listing online sources is different in different referencing styles, with some – like Harvard – requiring a notation that the source was found online [Online], and others allowing the citation of a URL or DOI to suffice. With Harvard, you will need to include the URL and/or the DOI and the most recent date that you accessed the website. Although most word-processing software automatically creates hyperlinks for URLs, you should always check that your hyperlinks are live, and accurate (that is, link to the right place).

Below you will find further examples of common academic sources, with common reference examples for printed and online forms.

Books

Abbreviated (in-text) reference
Single author:

(Marx, 1888, p. 15)

Note, however, that it is unlikely you will be working from an original 1888 copy. In the full reference, you will need to indicate the date of the modern edition you are actually using (see below for details on 'Different publication dates – modern editions').

Matthews notes that 'kittens are often delightful' (2010, ch. 6).

In this example, the eBook reader did not access page numbers, so the location of the direct quote is indicated as best as possible, by chapter. Where there are two authors – and no direct quotation – an example of the form for the abbreviated reference would be:

(Oosterveer and Sonnenfeld, 2012)

Where there are more than two authors, the abbreviated reference gives the first author's surname and then 'et al.' (meaning 'and others'):

(Frosh et al., 2002, p. 18)

Full reference, print, eBook and online

The full reference lists all the authors, in the order in which they appear in the work itself, which might not be alphabetically.

Print:

Frosh, S., Phoenix, A. and Pattman, P. (2002) *Young Masculinities: Understanding Boys in Contemporary Society*, London, Palgrave.

Oosterveer, P. and Sonnenfeld, D. (2014) *Food, Globalization and Sustainability*, London, Earthscan.

eBook (e.g. Kindle):

Marx, K. and Engels, F. (1888) *The Communist Manifesto* (eBook), New York, Bantam (this edition 2004).

Online:

Willie, S.S. (2003) *Acting Black: College, Identity and the Performance of Race* [Online], New York, Routledge. Available at http://library.open.ac.uk/linking/index.php?id=311027 (accessed 10 April 2010).

A further note about eBooks, books accessed online and PDFs

Some referencing formats no longer distinguish between eBooks and hard copy: Harvard does, however. Consequently, your full Harvard reference should indicate that your source is an eBook. The format for this is as follows:

Last name, First initial(s). (Year published) *Title*, Edition. [Format]. Publisher's location, Publisher, page(s). Available at URL (accessed date).

If we had read Castells as an eBook or downloaded it and read the PDF, the full reference would look like this:

Castells, M. (2015) *Networks of Outrage and Hope: Social Movements in the Internet Age*, 2nd edn. [PDF]. Chichester, Wiley and Sons. Available at https://books.google.co.uk/books?hl=en&lr=&id=ETHOCQAAQBAJ&oi=fnd&pg=PT7&ots=-ZAJvjmpwM&sig=gC6K663NeRhYccrS1H_23lQEAis#v=onepage&q&f=false (accessed 30 May 2016).

Note that the location and publisher have changed – in this case, the eBook and available PDF version are published by John Wiley and Sons rather than Polity Press who published the hard copy version we read.

Edited collection

This refers to a collection of chapters, articles or extracts compiled by one or more editors.

Abbreviated reference

If you simply refer to the book itself, treat the name(s) of the editor(s) as the author(s):

(Rochester et al., 2011)

or, if you are quoting directly or summarizing a specific argument, then include the page number:

(Rochester et al., 2011, p. ix)

Full reference

Editor(s) Last Name, First Initial(s). (ed(s)) (Year of publication) *Book Title*, Publisher's location, Publisher.

Example:

Rochester, C., Gosling, G.C., Penn, A. and Zimmeck, M. (eds) (2011) *Understanding the Roots of Voluntary Action: Historical Perspectives on Current Social Policy*, Brighton, Sussex Academic Press.

It is worth mentioning, however, that it is unusual to quote the editors of a book directly (unless from their introduction) or to cite an entire, edited collection. It is more common to cite a chapter *within* the book, in which case you should follow the instructions for chapters, articles or extracts, below.

Chapters, articles or extracts

If you are quoting from one of the chapters in an edited collection, the abbreviated reference should give the name(s) of the author(s) of that chapter and the date of the edited collection. For example, as well as being one of the editors of the above collection, Alison Penn also wrote one of its chapters.

Abbreviated reference

(Penn, 2011)

Full reference

Penn, A. (2011) 'Social History and Organizational Development: Revisiting Beveridge's *Voluntary Action*', in Rochester, C., Gosling, G.C., Penn, A. and Zimmeck, M. (eds) *Understanding the Roots of Voluntary Action: Historical Perspectives on Current Social Policy,* Brighton, Sussex Academic Press.

Some formats require that, in a full reference, you state the page numbers of chapters in edited collections in the same manner as articles in journals (see below). However, this practice is not uniform.

Journal/periodical article

As you progress in your studies, you will increasingly find yourself citing academic journals. Make sure you get these references right. They involve identifying the author(s) of the article as well as the name of the journal – this is not dissimilar to citing a chapter in an edited collection (such as the Penn example above).

Abbreviated reference

(Torfason and Ingram, 2010)

Or, if you are quoting directly, or summarizing a specific argument:

(Torfason and Ingram, 2010, p. 366)

More than two authors follows the same format as the book example, above:

(Willis et al., 2010, p. 250)

Full reference

For the full article within a journal reference you should include details of the journal volume and issue number and the page numbers between which the article appears, but you don't need to include the place of publication or publisher's name. For example:

Torfason, M.T. and Ingram, P. (2010) 'The global rise of democracy: A network account', *American Sociological Review*, vol. 75, no. 3, pp. 355–77.

Online journals/periodicals

Articles from online journals require some additional information. Sometimes it is enough to give the URL for the article, but depending on what sort of access you have to the journal (which will depend on such things as your university library's permissions, or whether the journal is a creative commons – 'CC' – journal), the direct URL may not work for others. If you know there is restricted access, it may be best to give the 'home page' URL for the journal, and then list the DOI:

Torfason, M.T. and Ingram, P. (2010) 'The global rise of democracy: A network account', *American Sociological Review*, vol. 75, no. 3, pp. 355–77 [Online]. Available at http://asr.sagepub.com/content/75/3/355.full, DOI: 10.1177/0003122410372230 (accessed 29 May 2016).

As with any online source, note that you should include the most recent date that you accessed the article. We have looked at this article a number of times, but most recently accessed it on 29 May 2016.

Dates and international conventions

As this book was written in the UK, the 'accessed' dates follow the standard of date/month/year (used in most of the world). However, US publications use the month/date/year standard, while other countries, such as China, use year/month/date. For this reason, it is wise to spell out the month name (e.g. October) and to give the full year (1963, rather than 63) to avoid confusion. Particularly if you are on an international course, you will be forgiven for getting the order 'back to front', but be consistent, whichever order you use.

Newspaper article

These follow much the same pattern as journal articles, although omitting in the full reference the page numbers between which the item appears.

Abbreviated reference

(McKibben, 2016)

Full reference

McKibben, B. (2016) 'The time has come to turn up the heat on those who are wrecking planet Earth', *Guardian*, 3 May, p. 5.

Notice that the full reference includes the specific date of publication after the newspaper's title.

Online full reference

Brown, Mark (2010) 'Linguist on mission to save Inuit "fossil language" disappearing with the ice', *Guardian*, 13 August [Online]. Available at www.guardian.co.uk/world/2010/aug/13/inuit-language-culture-threatened (accessed 29 May 2016).

Blogs

Harvard referencing for blogs is not dissimilar to that for online journals and follows the author/date format. One difference may be if the blogger uses an alias, in which case, the alias should be used instead of the author's name.

Abbreviated reference

(Weller, 2010)

Full reference

Author, A. (Year of publication/last updated) 'Title of message', *Title of Website*, blog entry posted day/month of posted message [Online], Available at URL (accessed date).

Weller, M. (2010) 'For the last time – open access is not like stealing bread', *The Ed Techie*, blog entry, 30 July [Online]. Available at http://nogoodreason.typepad.co.uk/no_good_reason/2010/07/for-the-last-time-open-access-is-not-like-stealingbread.html (accessed 13 August 2010).

Government/official publication

For the most part, government documents are published by Departments, who take the place of the 'author' in a standard reference. Occasionally, however, you will find a named author or researcher has been listed prominently on the document. If this is the case, the author/researcher name goes first. Also, while you may use some archive materials that are available in hard copy (see the full reference below), for the most part, you will access government papers and data online.

Abbreviated reference

(Department of Social Security, 1999)

Full reference

Department of Social Security (1999) 'Action across the UK', *Opportunity for All: Tackling Poverty and Social Exclusion,* London, The Stationery Office (September, Cm 4445).

Online full reference

House of Commons (2016) 'Older Women in the Workplace', *Hansard,* 26 May, Volume 611 [Online]. Available at https://hansard.parliament.uk/Commons/2016-05-26/debates/16052616000020/OlderWomenInThe Workplace (accessed 30 May 2016).

MacDonald, Z., Tinsley, L., Collingwood, J., Jamieson, P. and Pudney, S. (2005) 'Measuring the harm from illegal drugs using the Drug Harm Index', Home Office Report [Online], 24 May. Available at www.homeoffice.gov.uk/rds/pdfs05/rdsolr2405.pdf (accessed 28 May 2005).

Office for National Statistics (2013) 'What does the 2011 Census Tell Us About Older People?' [Online]. Available at www.ons.gov.uk/ons/rel/census/2011-census-analysis/what-does-the-2011-census-tell-us-about-older-people-/what-does-the-2011-census-tell-us-about-older-people--full-infographic.html (accessed 30 December 2015).

Non-governmental organization publications

As with most government publications, the 'author' is the institution, though where there is a named author or lead researcher(s), follow the format for author/book or, in the case of a series of documents, author/journal article. Again, while you might find some materials – such as pamphlets or archived documents – in hard copy, most NGO publications will be online.

Abbreviated reference

(British Psychological Society, 2003)

Full reference

British Psychological Society (2003) 'Child protection – protecting children and young people from abuse, harm and neglect: the responsibilities of chartered psychologists', Leicester, British Psychological Society.

Online full reference

Greenpeace (2010) 'Briefing – opportunities and challenges for off-shore wind power in Britain', London, Greenpeace [Online]. Available at www.green peace.org.uk/files/pdfs/climate/Outline_briefing_offshore_wind_20100114. pdf (accessed 13 August 2010).

Pew Research Center (2014) 'Older Adults and Technology Use' [Online]. Available at www.pewinternet.org/2014/04/03/older-adults-and-technology- use/ (accessed 29 December, 2015).

Online research project

Dunne, M., Humphreys, S. and Leach, F. (2003) 'Gender violence in school' [Online], School of Education, University of Sussex. Available at http:// portal.unesco.org/education/en/file_download.php/ee2258a3769cd087c c2453acdbe3910Genderandviolenceinschools.doc (accessed 19 May 2005).

Online conference paper

Hosu, A. (2003) 'Identity politics and narrativity', The Second Tampere Conference on Narrative, Tampere, 26–8 June [Online]. Available at www. uta.fi/conference/narrative/papers/hosu.pdf (accessed 19 May 2005).

Film, television or DVD

If you are doing a media studies or film degree, your course may have particular conventions for citing films, television or radio programmes and series. On many film courses, the director takes the place of the 'author'. However, if you are researching screenplays, you may find the convention of the screenwriter taking the 'author' place. You will notice that the Harvard format presented below deviates from the standard 'author/date' template, with the title of the film or television programme coming first, in *italics*.

Abbreviated reference

(Little Miss Sunshine, 2006)

(Peaky Blinders, 2016)

Full reference
For a film:

Title of Film (Year of distribution) Directed by Director Name [Medium, i.e. Film or DVD], Place of distribution, Distribution company.

Example:

Little Miss Sunshine (2006) Directed by Jonathan Dayton and Valerie Faris [Film], Burbank, Fox Searchlight.

For a television programme or series:

Title of the series or programme (Year of transmission) 'Title of episode' and/or Series number, episode number, Channel, date of transmission.

Example:

Peaky Blinders (2016) Series 4, Episode 2, BBC2, 12 May.

In this case, the episode did not have a title, so the number of the episode 'stands in'. Indeed, you may not be able to get all of the other information for some television or radio programmes. Ephemeral programmes, like the news or talk shows, may be referenced like this:

Title of the Series or Programme (Year of transmission) Channel, Date of broadcast.

Example:

The Daily Show with Jon Stewart (2010) More 4, 13 August (originally broadcast 12 August 2010).

In this case, the programme was a topical daily programme initially broadcast in the US; the version that is cited here is a 'repeat' transmission, broadcast in the UK a day later.

Online full reference
For a film, TV or radio programme accessed online the required information is a little different:

Title of the Series or Programme (Year of transmission) Channel [Online]. Available at URL (accessed date).

Example:

The Human Footprint (2010) Channel 4 On Demand [Online]. Available at www.channel4.com/programmes/the-human-footprint/4od (accessed 13 August 2010).

Podcasts/Downloads

The Harvard system for referencing podcasts is not dissimilar to that for film or TV programmes.

Abbreviated reference

(Thinking Allowed, 2016)

Full reference
The full reference format is as follows:

Title of podcast (Year of publication), Episode title (if available), Podcaster/Publisher, Date of transmission [Online]. Available at URL (accessed date).

Examples:

Thinking Allowed (2016) 'The Flaneur – Walking in the City', BBC Radio 4, 02 May [Online]. Available at www.bbc.co.uk/programmes/b0787dmb (accessed 30 May 2016).

Does Prison Work? (2010) iTunes [Video], The Open University, Milton Keynes (accessed 13 August 2010).

YouTube

YouTube clips are incredibly varied, of course, but broadly follow the film referencing format in the Harvard system.

Abbreviated reference

(Bert on how the internet has changed his life, 2010)

Full reference
The full reference format looks like this:

Title of Item (Year of distribution), YouTube [Video], added by name of who uploaded it. Available at URL (accessed date).

Example:

Bert on how the internet has changed his life (2010) YouTube [Video], added by raceonline2012. Available at www.youtube.com/watch?v=xVDBeK7U4P I&feature=channel (accessed 30 May 2016).

Online forums

In general, you will want to cite a particular message to a forum and should, therefore, identify the author. Before doing so, however, you must formally check that the author is happy for you to quote them. Notice that if there is a series of postings by the same author you should include the time of the posting as well as the date. If the forum is *public* rather than a closed group forum, you should also include the standard online information: Available at URL (accessed date).

Abbreviated reference

(Bhote, 2010)

Full reference

Last Name, Initial(s). (Year) 'Subject of message', forum message to Name of the Forum, date and time of posting.

Example:

Bhote, K. (2010) 'Twitter as a research tool', forum message to Tutor-group forum, H800 Technology-enhanced learning: practices and debates, 23 June 07:02.

10.5 Advanced referencing

In the preceding section we explored some of the referencing conventions that you are likely to use fairly frequently. In what follows, we will investigate a few more complex referencing issues.

An author quoted in another text

Sometimes you will come across a quotation or reference in a book you are reading and decide to reference it in your own work. In such circumstances it is good practice to find the original source to check that the details are correct (for example, has the original author been misquoted or her or his argument distorted?). However, particularly if the source is obscure, untranslated or long out of print, this may not be possible. For example, in her book *Feminism, Theory and the Politics of Difference* (1999), Chris Weedon quotes from an out-of-print book by Emma Drake, published in 1901, to illustrate the point that women's reproductive capacity has frequently been seen to define their gender. If we were to use this quotation ourselves, it is likely we would be unable to find the original source, so we make an accommodation.

Abbreviated reference

(Drake, quoted in Weedon, 1999, p. 7)

Full reference

Weedon, C. (1999) *Feminism, Theory and the Politics of Difference*, Oxford, Blackwell.

Specialist learning guides or audio-visual material

This refers to the support material that may come with your module or on your course. Material of this kind may also not have an identifiable 'author'. For example, for an Open University film, audio programme or assignment handbook, the 'author' should be identified as the university itself.

Abbreviated reference

(The Open University, 2005)

Full reference, for an audio programme, for instance

The Open University (2005) 'Powers and structures' [Audio], DD203 *Power, Dissent, Equality: Understanding Contemporary Politics*.

Were this audio accessed online, the URL and accessed date would also be included.

Personal communication

If you quote something said to you in a conversation or letter, you should reference this.

Abbreviated reference

(Toynbee, 2016)

Full reference

Toynbee, J. (2016) Personal email communication with author, 4 May.

If the quote is from correspondence between two other people, you should indicate this. Further details can include the email subject line, or if the posting is one of a series on a given date, you can include the time of the post:

Toynbee, J. (2016) 'Meeting time?' Email to Wendy Maples, 3 May, 08.24.

Different publication dates and modern editions

Different referencing styles have different conventions for indicating modern editions. In the Harvard style, you must first cite the original date of publication in the reference. For instance, *The German Ideology* – a key text in classical Marxist theory – first appeared in the nineteenth century. The in-text reference for this text is below.

Abbreviated reference

(Marx and Engels, 1846)

However, one edition of this text was published in 1974. Assuming this is the edition you are using, the full reference will need to indicate that your copy of the book is the more recent.

Full reference

Marx, K. and Engels, F. (1846) *The German Ideology*, London, Lawrence and Wishart (this edition 1974).

Where dates for reprints are noted, use the year given against the copyright (©) line.

Modern editions and citing page numbers

For specific points, including quotations from an early work, it is crucial that you clearly indicate the date of the newer edition in the full reference, as page numbers cited in the essay will refer to this edition. The in-text reference will look like this:

(Marx and Engels, 1846, p. 26)

Publisher and place of publication

Assuming that you are writing in Britain or for a British audience, you need to quote the British place of publication of British publishers. For example, Sage is based in London, so you put London as the place of publication. If you are writing in the USA, for a US audience, you should give the US address of the publisher if there is one. Sage, for example, also has a base in Thousand Oaks, California – so Thousand Oaks becomes the place of publication. Be sure to give the place of publication (that is, the city or town where the publisher is based) and not the place where the book was printed.

Collaborative publishing

Sometimes books, television series or online courses will be co-published. Many university course books are collaborations of this kind. In such cases, name both publishers. The place(s) of publication will be indicated on the imprint page.

Abbreviated reference

(Andrews and Saward, 2005)

Full reference

Andrews, G. and Saward, M. (eds) (2005) *Living Political Ideas*, Edinburgh/Milton Keynes, Edinburgh University Press/The Open University.

10.6 Compiling your references

It's a good idea to familiarize yourself with the basic principles for writing references before you begin to access your sources. Then, *at the time* you are researching your sources, keep to hand this chapter. Note down all the details you will require including page numbers for journal and newspaper articles, and the exact page number for any quotes or key ideas you think you might use. It is also good practice to note down where you found your material: Google Scholar, the local library, borrowed from a friend, etc., in case you need to find it again. Almost all of us have at some time omitted to note our references properly and learned how difficult it is to trace the reference details afterwards – usually at the very moment that the essay is due to be handed in.

As already noted, there are a number of referencing software packages, such as EndNote Basic (http://endnote.com/product-details/basic) or RefMe (www.refme.com), or your university might have its own package as part of its student support or library facilities. Different software will translate your citations into a range of citation styles, store your notes and quotes, and/or alphabetize your citations automatically. Some use key word or tag functions to help you keep different lists of references for different purposes. You would be well advised to make use of such facilities from the beginning of your studies.

In terms of producing your references for an essay, perhaps the best advice is to try to remember the basic referencing format and then look up the further guidance details as you need them. Certainly you should not be intimidated by what looks like a complex process. Get started on the basics, using the guidance above, and then check the specific examples as the need arises.

Summary

- Referencing is a basic academic skill and it is almost certain that you will be expected to use references accurately on undergraduate courses.
- To write a reference using the Harvard system you should give an abbreviated reference in the text and full details in a list of references at the end of the text.
- Abbreviated references in the text are written: (Author's last name, publication date). If you are using a direct quote or specific point, you will also need to include the page number: (Author's last name, publication date, page number).
- Full references at the end of the text are listed alphabetically by author (or editor, etc.).
- References for different publications by the same author in the same year are distinguished using 'a', 'b', etc., according to the order in which they appear in the essay.
- Where the same author has produced multiple cited works, these should be listed in reverse chronological order.

(Continued)

(Continued)

- Full references at the end of the text for a single author book are written: Author's surname and Initial(s), publication date, *Title* (italicized or underlined), Place of publication, Publisher. Electronic references follow similar principles as those for printed texts but must also indicate they are an online source [Online] and include the URL and date of access.
- References to chapters in edited collections, to journal and newspaper articles, and to various other sources are given in slightly different ways. Titles of chapters, journal and newspaper articles are given in quotes: 'Distinctiveness and difference with New Labour'.
- Note down your reference details at the time you are finding your material, including where you located the book/article/programme.
- Various software packages are available, possibly through your university, that can help with a range of referencing issues, including translating between referencing styles, storing and ordering notes, quotes and citations.

Self-test

1 Why is referencing important?
2 What style of referencing should you adopt for your essays? (Answer: whichever system is recommended on your course or by your tutor.)
3 What resources might you use to help you with producing your referencing in the right format?
4 Using the Harvard system, what is the basic format for: an abbreviated (in-text) reference and a full (reference list) reference?

Don't forget! Visit https://study.sagepub.com/redmanandmaples5 for more tasks and resources related to this chapter.

11

Essay-writing Skills and Other Forms of Social Science Writing

- Academic essays and other critical writing
- Why an essay is not a news article or report
- Using essay-writing skills in other forms of written assessment

Essays have much in common with other forms of academic and other public writing. There are, however, also important differences. This chapter teases out some of the similarities and differences between, for instance, essays and reports, and describes how some of the skills of essay writing can be utilised in other academic assessments.

11.1 Academic essays and other critical writing

The standard format for essays – an introduction, main section with a series of arguments, supported by empirical evidence, and a conclusion – is a format that appears not just in undergraduate essays but is distinctive. As well as having a particular structure, however, the essay's distinctiveness is also to do with 'academic register' or 'voice'. As you become a stronger essay writer you will develop a 'voice' that is your own, but one that conforms to the conventions of academic practice. For social scientists, this practice includes the use of evidence to support an argument, and providing references that show where your ideas and evidence have come from. It also includes the ability to write with some confidence, using the specialist language of your subject area.

We have included extracts from academic journal articles throughout this book, which perhaps have the most in common with university student essays. Some periodicals, however, such as *The London Review of Books, The Atlantic* or *The New Yorker*, critically explore political and cultural issues in articles which use a form that is very similar to an academic essay. Some 'magazine-style' television or radio programmes also formulate particular episodes or segments in what might be seen as an essay style – though arguably these owe a greater debt to speech and debate than to the written essay. However, great speeches – and some debating styles – broadly follow an essay format. The point is that the standard essay we have explored in *Good Essay Writing* is a powerful, tried and tested format that enables complex, detailed and sophisticated ideas to be expressed with clarity: not surprisingly, therefore, the distinctive essay style appears in academic and other critically-engaged public works.

11.2 Why an essay is not a news article or a report

Conforming to the essay's basic conventions around how to present ideas and arguments helps us more easily compare those ideas, just as conforming to the rules of a game makes it easier for one sports team to play against another. If one team is playing cricket and the other baseball, we will find there are similarities (both use bats, have innings, make runs), but there will also be lots of awkward differences (LBW; sliding into home) – which are as much about style as they are about substance, but no less significant for that.

For many students information about the social, political and economic world comes from news articles accessed through newspapers or websites. Some students will come from professional backgrounds where report writing is a common form of communication. News articles and reports are legitimate forms of writing that serve useful purposes – but they aren't essays.

News articles

For many students, journalistic styles of writing are the most familiar styles of writing. Catchy headlines (or titles) are appealing, and news articles' to-the-point presentation may make for easier reading. News stories, however, follow a different set of requirements to essays – a different set of 'golden rules' (see section 2.4). In general, website and newspaper articles foreground the 'who, what, where, when and why' of a story in the first paragraph. The most important information is despatched immediately, with the assumption that all readers will read the headline, most readers will read the first paragraph, and dwindling numbers will read the remainder of the article. Everyday news articles often finish with a whimper for this reason, and there may be no attempt to summarize findings or provide a conclusion at the end – that's not the role of news journalists. (Though there is quite a different set of rules for 'Op Ed' or opinion pieces, or longer feature articles.) Student essays, by contrast, should be structured to be read from beginning to end, with the ideas and arguments building up to a strong conclusion.

Of course, there are also similarities. The main sections of broadsheet papers will be concerned with matters that are also of interest to social scientists – such as the 'differences that make a difference'. Credible news articles will be based on sound research and will introduce evidence and reference 'who said what'.

Reports

Reports can take a variety of forms, but typically involve an up-front 'executive summary' and a series of discussions, usually with numbered headings and sub-headings. They are also likely to include 'bullet points' that capture an idea or argument in a succinct way. Professional reports may include evidence, arguments, recommendations and references. You may already have spotted some of the similarities with essays – and the crucial differences. Let's begin with the similarities. Reports and essays both involve discussion, the use of evidence to support (or refute) a claim, argument or proposal, and a list of references. Both will have an introductory section, a main body, and a conclusion. However, the differences are important. With the exception of very long essays (dissertations and the like), essays do not generally have numbered headings and sub-headings. Nor do they have bullet points. They also don't have executive summaries. And, with some notable exceptions (such as essays around areas of social policy perhaps), social science essays don't usually require you to produce policy recommendations.

11.3 Using essay-writing skills in other forms of written assessment

Your course may require you to produce a range of assessed work, including perhaps reports or journalistic-style articles. Below we look at examples of other academic assignments – the reflective essay, wiki entries, small-scale research projects and exam answers – and consider how the skills of essay writing can help you produce better writing in these other formats.

Reflective essays

Reflective writing will 'feel different' from the kind of objective or detached writing that is more conventional in other social science essays. With reflective prose, you will frequently use the first person pronoun (see sections 12.2 and 12.3), perhaps to describe an observation ('I saw'), to set out considerations ('I wondered') or to indicate courses of action ('I decided'), and will engage with what your tutors may describe as 'affective learning'. In other words, you will consider how you *processed* the experience of learning and will then need to put this into words.

A short piece of reflective writing is now often required of students immediately following submission of a formal social science essay, in the form of a reflection about what was most difficult or most easily achievable about the assignment. This reflective practice (whether required or not) is extremely helpful in developing essay writing, as it helps you become more conscious of your strengths and weaknesses (much in the same way reflecting on essay feedback can do – see section 3.2).

A full reflective essay is, however, something rather more, and has similarities and differences with conventional social science essays. Reflective essays are likely to be framed around a social science area of interest (e.g. 'differences that make a difference') or contention (on applied social science courses, this is likely to be around social policy). Structurally, a reflective essay will include the conventions of an introduction, main body and conclusion, and will most likely require a reference list that includes academic texts. However, what 'counts' for evidence in a reflective essay is somewhat different. According to Gillie Bolton, ' … reflective stories are based on direct experience, exploring and making sense of identity, memories, understandings and feeling' (Bolton, 2014, p. 71). Consequently, evidence may include notations on observations, quotations from conversations, or selected passages from a reflective journal. As with conventional essays, evidence will need to 'work' to support or refute claims or discussion points and, as with conventional essays, such evidence will need to be properly cited and referenced.

It is important to dispel the notion that the reflective essay is primarily descriptive. In fact, being self-reflexive about what is, for instance, experienced or observed, the method of observation and how your theoretical perspective might shape your understanding of your observation, or considering the experiences and perspective of others, means that a reflective essay, like a conventional social sciences essay, can – and at the higher levels will – involve critical thinking, including analysis and evaluation.

Wiki entries

Your tutor may ask you to contribute to a wiki either individually or as part of a collaborative assignment with other students. In section 5.3, we explored the 'perils' and 'pleasures' of the internet and considered the particular issues associated with using Wikipedia as a main source of essay material. At its best, Wikipedia (and other wikis) provide a platform for accumulating and sharing knowledge and understanding on a particular topic. This aim of accumulating and sharing knowledge and understanding is not dissimilar to the aim of an essay. At their best, wiki entries draw on thinking and evidence that stand up to (public) scrutiny and provide links to authoritative documentation. This is not dissimilar to the criteria used for including (peer-reviewed) evidence and theories in an essay or academic journal article. The best wiki entries are well structured, guiding the reader through the topic, using clear 'signposting' or explaining unfamiliar terminology. Though wikis are generally structured more like reports, perhaps you can see how essay-writing skills – such as conducting a literature review, note-taking, using evidence, structuring an argument – might help you create a wiki entry?

Research projects

There are many books written for students on how to conduct a research project, and if you are asked to undertake research, you would do well to refer to the more detailed advice you will find there. There are, however, key areas of overlap between the kind of preparatory activity required for a small-scale research project and an essay that we will cover briefly.

The most obvious similarity is the need for a literature review and other forms of evidence gathering (see section 5.3). Before setting out on your own research, you will need to find out what other research on your topic or issue has already been conducted, and what relevant academic papers have already been published. You may want to find out if there are existing data such as population statistics from the Census, or if there are NGOs working in the same or related fields. You will, of course, need to take notes, compile them in a way that means you can access them easily, and ensure that you are using a good system for keeping and organizing your references.

Structurally too, you will probably find that your research illuminates a number of important points: in order to avoid getting 'lost' in your project, you will need to decide – as you would with the main body of a conventional essay – which are the most vital, or, pragmatically, which areas are most promising in terms of finding enough useful material, and prioritize these (see section 3.3).

Lastly, you may be asked to write a formal essay about your project once you have completed your research. Keeping careful notes, ensuring your references are in order, being selective with your main points, and identifying the strongest evidence as you conduct your research will help you produce a stronger essay at the end of the project.

Exam writing

There are exam conventions that make exam writing – even 'essay-style' exams – different from essay writing, but there are also similarities, and there are ways in which essay-writing skills can help improve exam answers.

Perhaps the main differences are these: under exam conditions, it is understood that you are writing at speed and that you may not communicate as effectively as in a planned essay, and you will generally not be expected to provide formal citations (although you may be expected to link clearly authors and ideas).

You will, however, need to demonstrate your ability to use social science ideas and theories, the accepted terminology or 'jargon' of your subject area, and evidence to support or refute the argument being posed. Thinking critically and being selective about which theories will serve your purposes best, and which is the stronger evidence will help your answer.

Longer exam answers, which may be described as 'essay-style' answers, will also have structural similarities to an essay. You will need to include a short introduction, a main body of argument and discussion, with three or four main points, supported with evidence, and a conclusion. Shorter answers may have only a one-sentence introduction that perhaps simply reformulates the question in order to set out the direction of your answer, and may, similarly, have just a summary sentence for a conclusion. Very short exam answers might not resemble essays at all as they may focus on a single piece of factual knowledge or very brief points of comparison, and will necessarily dispense with any introduction or conclusion.

Summary

- Social science essay writing is distinct from other forms of writing such as reports or news articles.
- Essay writing is distinctive in terms of its style as well as its substance.
- Other forms of written assessment may draw on the conventions of good essay-writing practice

Self-test

1 What distinguishes a social science essay from a news article or a report?
2 What essay-writing conventions are drawn upon in other forms of written assessment?
3 What essay-writing skills might help you: write a reflective essay or wiki entry, conduct a research project, or produce an essay-style exam answer?

Don't forget! Visit **https://study.sagepub.com/redmanandmaples5** for more tasks and resources related to this chapter.

12

Some Common Worries

- Writing too much or too little
- Using the 'I' word, subjectivity and objectivity
- Using your own experience
- Presentation, spelling, grammar and punctuation
- Plagiarism and poor academic practice

It is difficult to predict all the worries that you may have in writing essays. But there are a few important points to know about and some things to avoid, so read this chapter carefully.

12.1 Writing too much or too little

Most essays have word limits. Many students point out that they could easily write a whole lot more on any one topic. Indeed, people write 80,000-word books on the sort of issues that you address in your essays, so everyone knows that word limits can be rather restrictive. However, they are not set merely to irritate you. Shorter essays are an important academic tool. In writing them, you learn how to prioritize and select material, and how to condense big topics into a punchy, easily digested form. These are academic skills that you will need even in writing much longer pieces. Painful though it may be, if you're writing too much, be ruthless. Concentrate on the biggest, most important arguments and examples – and cut the rest. Your work will almost certainly be better for it.

Remember that on many courses you will need to provide a word count at the end of your essay and that marks may be deducted if you have exceeded this (always check the regulations covering the specific course that you are studying). Furthermore, some markers may feel that writing over length allows you to cover a topic in more detail than other people and thus confers an unfair advantage on you.

If, on the other hand, you find it difficult to fill the page, it is essential to ask yourself whether you are addressing the question adequately – whether there is enough depth or breadth to your answer, or whether you have pro-vided appropriate support for your argument in the form of examples or illustrations. Re-read the assignment question (and any guidance notes) for clues as to what might be 'missing'. If your essay is too short, it may also be the case that you have not written an essay, but have instead produced a report or other condensed written form.

12.2 Using the 'I' word, 'subjectivity' and 'objectivity'

There are no hard and fast rules about using 'I' in social science essays, and different disciplines (and different tutors) tend to adopt different conven-tions. Perhaps the best way to find out whether the use of 'I' is appropriate to the particular course you are studying is to check with the person marking your work. Sometimes you will be told that the first-person pronoun ('I') should be avoided (for example, that you should not write 'In this essay I intend to explore ... '). In this case, you can often ignore personal pronouns completely (for example, by writing 'This essay will explore ... ').

'I' is sometimes thought to indicate a lack of objectivity, but it is important to separate out the different issues here. It is possible to be objective and use the first-person pronoun. It is possible to be utterly subjective in your writing without using 'I' at all. Phrases including 'I think', 'I believe' and 'I feel', how-ever, risk you making assertions without offering evidence or developing a logical argument – and this is the real concern for social science writing. Some social scientists argue that it is better to be upfront about our subject positions or investments in a topic. For instance, the introduction to *Good Essay Writing* might have mentioned that our 'investment' in writing this book is because we've seen students enjoy being able to express themselves better and more easily after they've been given a few clear pointers on essay writing. This doesn't make the book or its suggestions less valid, but it does help you understand why we've written it.

In a reflective essay (see section 11.3) you will of course use 'I'. You will also use 'I' when your essay evidence includes personal observations. Where you are asked for some self-reflection on your experience of doing the assignment it is generally accepted that you will reflect using the first-person pronoun. Even in these cases, however, you will want to avoid the excessive repetition of 'I' – as with any other word or phrase.

12.3 Using your own experience

Some essay questions will explicitly ask you to draw on your personal experience – indeed, autobiography and autoethnography are recognized research methods in the social sciences: reflective or personal observations can develop rich insights into the social. Additionally, relevant personal experience can sometimes be used to add 'colour' to an argument or to grab the reader's attention.

Having said this, there can be a danger that – in the context of social scientific writing – personal experience will sound like barroom philosophy. In other words, it will be little more than unsubstantiated personal opinion. A good rule therefore is to avoid the use of personal experience in academic writing unless you are explicitly asked to do otherwise (see section 11.3).

12.4 Presentation, spelling, grammar and punctuation

Your essays will be marked first and foremost on their content, however your work should also be well-presented (see also section 3.4). Your course or module may have specific presentation conventions, but in general you should ensure that in the header for each page you include:

- your name and/or personal identifier;
- the module or course number and the assignment number/name;
- the name of your tutor;
- the date of submission.

In addition, you should have a title, either on a title page or at the top of page 1, and each page should be numbered, including the reference list page, but *excluding* the title page if you are asked for this.

Correct spelling, grammar and punctuation are part of a good presentation – and are important in essay writing. The baseline here is that essays should be readable and make sense. Your spelling, grammar and punctuation need to be good enough to communicate effectively to your reader, and at degree level or its equivalent this implies the ability to use conventions of spelling, grammar and punctuation accurately.

As a result, you should choose your words carefully in order to say what you mean – and mean what you say. Use of 'jargon' words has already been mentioned in 'Clear sentences and paragraphs' (in section 8.4). If you use abbreviations or foreign words, make sure you use them correctly (Appendix B has a list of those commonly found). To help you with standard English words, you should have a dictionary (Chambers, Oxford or Webster's are all good) to hand (don't rely on spell check), and you may also find it helpful to have a style guide, such as *The Oxford A–Z of Grammar and Punctuation* (Seely, 2013), to help with solving a variety of writing dilemmas, such as when to use a colon or semi-colon, or whether the full stop (period) should go inside or outside the close brackets (parentheses). For a more light-hearted and enjoyably zealous approach to grammar and punctuation, you might also find Lynne Truss's *Eats, Shoots and Leaves: The Zero Tolerance Approach to Punctuation* (Truss, 2009) both helpful and enjoyable.

It is good practice to read aloud, to yourself or a trusted peer, the whole of your essay. If you stumble in reading, this may be an indication that a sentence is not as clear as it might be. You may also ask someone else to read your work before you submit it: often a fresh set of eyes will catch errors that you have missed. This is generally considered to be good practice and is why professional writers have editors. One further point – a trusted peer is *not* someone who will tell you everything you've written is marvellous. Ideally, you should ask someone who is willing to be politely critical of your work, remembering that they are commenting on the essay, not on you personally.

12.5 Plagiarism and poor academic practice

The whole of this guide is premised on supporting good academic practice and helping you avoid poor academic practice. Poor academic practice includes things like not answering the question, failing to follow your tutor's guidance, writing incoherent sentences or over-using colloquial phrases, insufficient research, superficial reading, etc. However, possibly the greatest bugbear for teachers in higher education is the poor academic practice of plagiarism.

Plagiarism means using someone else's work and passing it off as your own. It refers to copying other people's work word for word, or making only minor changes to it with the intention of representing their words as yours. This does not mean that you are forbidden to use any word or phrase that appears in a text from which you are working. In particular, you will almost certainly need to repeat technical vocabulary. For example, it would look rather odd if an essay on Marxist theory avoided key conceptual categories such as 'class struggle' or 'relation to the means of production'. The problem occurs when you recycle whole sentences or paragraphs without indicating that these are quotations, or paraphrased from your original source.

Sometimes plagiarism is clear cut and easily recognizable – but sometimes it is the result of other poor academic practices. Of course, it is easy enough to avoid intentionally passing off someone else's work as your own. However, some students seem to copy or closely paraphrase other people's work without realizing.

There are, perhaps, three main reasons why students sometimes plagiarize inadvertently:

- bad note-taking, including poor referencing
- lack of confidence
- a failure to understand what it means to 'write in your own words'.

The first two are fairly easy to address. Bad note-taking can lead to inadvertent plagiarism when, in preparing for an essay, students copy material into their notes without using quotation marks or references. This material then risks being transferred directly into the final essay, which in consequence will be partially – if inadvertently – plagiarized. This can be exacerbated when using sources that allow you to cut and paste, and even more so sources like Wikipedia which may themselves be inadequately referenced (see section 5.3). The solution of course is always to use quotation marks, and to record references when making notes (see section 5.2).

Lack of confidence can result in inadvertent plagiarism when students stick very closely to the original wording of a source because they are unsure of its exact meaning. In such circumstances, they may feel that copying or close paraphrasing reduces the risk of 'getting it wrong'. The problem is that the marker won't be able to tell how much the students have understood, and in consequence won't be able to award them many (if any) marks. The solution in this case is to take time to ensure that you fully understand what you are writing about and, when necessary, to ask for help from your tutor and/ or fellow students. Although it may seem pedestrian, you should also try to express ideas *as you understand them*. Particularly at the earlier stages of your studies, it may be more pedagogically productive not to use all of the academic vocabulary introduced on your course – at least until you feel more confident of its meaning.

Failure to understand what it means to 'write in your own words' is perhaps more complicated and requires a more detailed response.

What does it mean to 'write in your own words'?

In order to answer this question we need to look at some worked examples. These, and the commentary that accompanies them, are drawn from The Open University study support material, 'Writing in your own words' (Redman, 2002).

Imagine that you need to use the following invented conversation between two students for an essay on issues in teaching and learning social science. You need to distil their different positions, and represent these accurately, but in your own words.

Becky: 'I don't know why I decided to do this course. It's all jargon and theory and none of it makes any sense.

Elsie: Really? I like all the debates and the jargon is just like learning another language, but one that's useful, not like Latin.

Becky: Latin is infinitely more useful than, I don't know, Baudrillard. The Gulf War never happened? What does that mean? And anyway, it happened twice.

Elsie: I think Baudrillard meant that on the one hand the war wasn't a war in the sense that two powers were fighting over territory or a political ideal, but that we just treated it like a war because there were armies involved and bombs and destruction. On the other hand, for most people the 'experience' of the war was only representation – what they saw on TV. There's also the thing of euphemisms, so there's 'collateral damage', which actually means that a village has been bombed and civilians have died.

Becky: More jargon!

Elsie: Well, sort of. I mean what Baudrillard is saying is that it is all euphemism and representation, that all we can ever know is what we understand through signs and representation. The example of the Gulf War is used to explore how things have reached a kind of peak of 'hyper-reality', divorced from the real, visceral nature of war.

Becky: I can sort of see that. Like how during the Vietnam War the government suddenly realized that showing American soldiers coming back in body bags wasn't winning sympathy from the rest of America for the action in Vietnam; instead it was turning people against the idea of war altogether.

Elsie: I think I see what you're saying –

Becky: So, the point is that the government then tried to clean up the image of the war – and not let the news programmes show the coffins being unloaded from the planes, but the damage was already done: public opinion had already shifted. So you're saying that Baudrillard is pointing out that the news is so sanitized now that it is hard to imagine what's really going on. That it is just a simulacrum?

Elsie: I thought you hated 'jargon' ...

(Word count: 363)

Below you will find two versions of this dialogue, rewritten for inclusion in an essay.

Version A

A discussion between two students, Elsie and Becky, focused on the issue of social science 'jargon'. Becky found the concepts used by theorists such as Baudrillard obfuscating rather than illuminating. Elsie, however, was able to give a mainly accurate gloss of the main issues and some of the key terms in Baudrillard's article 'The Gulf War did not take place' (1991) and his assertion that symbols have become more real than reality – which he terms 'hyper-reality'. Although Becky misunderstood Elsie's description somewhat, suggesting Baudrillard was concerned with governments' attempts at fabrication, she found herself using his concept of the 'simulacrum' to clarify her point, perhaps undermining her claim that she was unhappy with the 'jargon' on her course.

(Word count: 118)

What does this tell us about 'writing in your own words'? You can see that the paragraph summarizes the main points of Elsie and Becky's discussion, but in the context of a set essay. The summary broadly follows the order of the discussion – though often you will find that it is necessary to shift around the key points. Having said this, it is also clear that, while the paragraph remains true to the original discussion, the vocabulary is substantially different and some less relevant points and details have been omitted. In addition, a note about the source Elsie has drawn upon has been made (Baudrillard's article, 'The Gulf War did not take place'). This is important because students sometimes think that 'writing in your own words' simply means taking a paragraph from a source and changing the odd word, omitting a couple of phrases, or rearranging a number of sentences.

For instance, instead of Version A above, another student might have come up with the following, rather problematic, summary:

Version B

Students Becky and Elsie discussed their social science course, Baudrillard and the problems with jargon. Becky said 'it's all jargon and theory and none of it makes sense'. Elsie pointed out that Baudrillard's ideas about the Gulf War are actually helpful: 'what Baudrillard is saying is that it is all euphemism and representation, that all we can ever know is what we understand through signs and representation. The example of the Gulf War is used to explore how things have reached a kind of peak of "hyper-reality", divorced from the real, visceral nature of war'. Becky didn't quite understand the point that Elsie made, but gave an interesting example of the way the US government tried to control the news of the Vietnam War. In the end, though, she used the term 'simulacrum', suggesting she was starting to feel happier about the use of 'jargon' in her course.

(Word count: 148)

If you compare Version B to the original extract you will see that, although it is not always copied word for word, it follows the original very closely, keeping the same order of the argument, using much of the same vocabulary and so on. In addition, it uses two direct quotes that take up a significant number of words: more problematically, neither helps the reader see whether the author understands the material. While this example wouldn't be seen as plagiarism, it is certainly poor academic practice and would not be awarded many marks, despite accurately recounting some parts of the dialogue.

As we saw in Version A, writing in your own words is very different from this. Rather than copying, it involves reflecting on and digesting someone else's ideas, and then producing your own interpretation of these and/or reworking them so that they address the specific task in hand (for example, answering a specific essay question).

Why is avoiding plagiarism so important?

It is important to get on top of this issue for a number of reasons. Most obviously, plagiarized work is likely to attract a fail grade. However, plagiarizing work is also of little educational benefit to you. The process of putting arguments into your own words is a crucial part of grasping ideas and committing them to memory. It also helps you learn how to use and apply the ideas for *yourself*. Plagiarizing, if nothing else, is a waste of your time since it probably means that you have not thoroughly understood what you have written.

Occasionally some people will deliberately plagiarize in an essay. This is a serious offence, since it is a form of academic theft. In the case of assessed coursework, it is also an attempt to gain qualifications by cheating. Many universities now use plagiarism detection software which identifies essays or sections of essays that replicate material found on a range of websites, or compare students' essays with one another. But tutors often note just how easy it is to spot plagiarism or poor academic practice. How? Tell-tale signs are things like a change of 'voice' (style or vocabulary) from one paragraph to the next, a distinctive turn of phrase from a well-known author, changes in typeface or font, or essays or sections of essays that relate to the broad topic, but don't answer the question, or don't answer it using the recommended texts from the course.

Tutors may be sympathetic in the first instance to inadvertent plagiarism, and may offer support to develop good academic practice; deliberate plagiarism, however, will almost certainly result in a fail mark and may incur further disciplinary penalties, with serious cases sometimes resulting in expulsion from university.

Summary

- Writing to a word limit is an important academic skill: it teaches you to condense complex material into its component parts, to select and communicate core arguments logically and with appropriate evidence or illustrations.
- Using 'I' is not the same as being subjective, but it can lead to poor social science practice. You should ask your tutor if use of the first-person pronoun is appropriate on your course.
- Personal experience can be a useful source of evidence and some courses or specific assignments (such as reflective essays or observations) will require you to use it. However, be careful to relate it to the course and the essay question and to substantiate your claims.
- Essays are expected to be well presented, readable, and to use conventions of spelling, grammar and punctuation correctly.
- Plagiarism is often unintentional and the result of poor academic practice. However, it is your responsibility to take clear notes, putting ideas and arguments into your own words and quotations in quotation marks or indented; to re-read your essays, looking for sudden changes in style or tone; and to seek help if you do not understand particular points to ensure that, when writing, you can reproduce them in your own words.
- Plagiarism means copying someone else's work and claiming it as your own. Plagiarized essays will normally attract a fail grade. Deliberate plagiarism, which constitutes cheating, may result in disciplinary action.

Self-test

1 How can you ensure you don't write 'too much' or 'too little'?
2 How is using the first-person pronoun different from being subjective, in social science terms?
3 In what sorts of academic writing would you be expected to use 'I'?
4 How can you ensure your grammar, spelling and punctuation are all correct?
5 What is plagiarism and why is it best avoided?
6 What are some of the strategies you can use to avoid plagiarism in your writing?

Don't forget! Visit **https://study.sagepub.com/redmanandmaples5** for more tasks and resources related to this chapter.

13

What Tutors Look for When Marking Essays

- Marking schemes: criteria related to grade bands
- Writing skills: 'introductory', 'intermediate' and 'advanced' essays

One of the most frequent and reasonable questions that students ask is, 'What should I be doing to get a better grade?' As you know, the answer to this question will depend on a number of factors. For example, what is required of an essay answer will vary according to the precise question set. Equally, the standard expected of essay writing is likely to be higher on more advanced undergraduate courses than on those at entry level. Similarly, there may be higher expectations towards the end of a module than there were at its start. Having said this, it is possible to specify the various qualities (if only in general terms) that distinguish essays in different grade bands, and what writing skills may be expected from essays at different levels.

Health warning

This chapter has been included to give you a *broad indication of what may be expected, in general, for different grades*. In the UK, grade bands are often defined in relation to 'learning outcomes' that draw on specified 'subject benchmarks' and 'key skills' (see for example www.qaa.ac.uk). In many countries, subject boards, formed from the relevant professional bodies, will provide colleges and universities with indices of knowledge and understanding in their field. Individual courses or modules will have specific requirements for each of the grade ranges. These requirements will vary depending on whether a module is at a more or less advanced stage of university study. As a result, where they are available, you may want to look at the learning outcomes specified for your particular course or module. However, you should remember that grading an essay is always a matter of weighing up not only the structure, content and style of the essay, but also the interplay between these, together with the interplay between any number of the different intellectual challenges built into the assignment. For all these reasons you should not expect the grading criteria for a specific module to map exactly onto what is set out here.

13.1 Marking schemes: criteria related to grade bands

In this chapter you will find guidelines adapted from those produced by the British Psychological Society (BPS, 1994) in conjunction with the Association of Heads of Psychology Departments and information from across a range of university institutions worldwide. These guidelines do not correspond to the specific policy of any specific higher education institution, but they should give you an idea of the sorts of *general* things markers are likely to consider for different grade ranges. Remember, what is expected for a particular module for a particular grade may differ from these guidelines. Remember also that you won't have to do well in every area to get a particular grade. For example, your depth of insight into theoretical issues may compensate for slightly weaker coverage of the evidence, or your understanding of the material may compensate for weaknesses in the coherence of your argument. It may also be the case that some of these criteria will be more relevant to advanced courses of undergraduate study (see section 13.2 below).

An essay in the top band (excellent pass, Table 13.1) will meet or exceed the very highest expectations for the assignment and is likely to:

- provide a comprehensive and accurate response to the question, demonstrating a breadth and depth of reading and understanding of relevant arguments and issues;
- show a sophisticated ability to synthesize a wide range of material;
- show a sophisticated ability to outline, analyse and contrast complex competing positions and to evaluate their strengths and weaknesses effectively;
- develop a sophisticated argument, demonstrating logical reasoning and the effective use of well-selected examples and evidence;
- demonstrate depth of insight into theoretical issues;

Table 13.1   Different grade bands and their equivalents

Descriptor	UK university		US university		Other				
Excellent Pass	1st	70+	A	4.0	85+	10	Perfect	Distinction
			A–	3.7		9	Very good	
Good Pass	2:1	60–69	B	3.0	70–84	8	Good	Merit
			B–	2.7		7	More than sufficient	
Clear Pass	2:2	50–59	C	2.0	55–69	6	Sufficient	Credit
			C–	1.7				
Bare Pass	3rd	40–49	D	1.0	40–54	5	Nearly sufficient	Pass
Bare Fail	Fail	30–39	F	0.0	30–39	4	Insufficient	Fail
						3	Strongly insufficient	
Clear Fail	Fail	0–29	F		15–29	2	Poor	Fail
Bad Fail					0–14	1	Very Poor	

- where appropriate, demonstrate an ability to apply ideas to new material or in a new context;
- demonstrate an ability to write from 'within' a perspective or theory, including the ability to utilize appropriate social scientific concepts and vocabulary;
- show a creative or original approach (within the constraints of academic rigour);
- demonstrate clarity of argument and expression, in the author's own words;
- use a standard referencing system accurately.

A good pass will meet most of the higher expectations of the assignment and is likely to:

- provide an accurate and well-informed answer to the question;
- be reasonably comprehensive;
- demonstrate an ability to synthesize a range of material;
- show an ability to outline, analyse and contrast more complex competing positions, and to evaluate their strengths and weaknesses effectively;
- demonstrate an ability to develop a strong and logical line of argument, supported by appropriate examples and evidence;
- demonstrate the ability to work with theoretical material effectively;
- demonstrate confidence in handling social scientific concepts and vocabulary;

- where appropriate, demonstrate an ability to apply ideas to new material or in a new context;
- be well organized and structured;
- demonstrate general clarity of argument and expression, and be written in the author's own words
- use a standard referencing system accurately, though perhaps with minor typographical errors.

A clear pass will meet all of the basic expectations of the assignment and is likely to:

- provide an adequate answer to the question, though one dependent on commentaries, secondary texts or a limited range of source material;
- be generally accurate, although with some omissions and minor errors;
- develop and communicate a basic logical argument with some use of appropriate supporting examples and evidence;
- demonstrate an ability to outline, analyse and contrast competing positions, and to begin to evaluate their strengths and weaknesses (although this may be derivative);
- demonstrate a basic ability to address theoretical material and to use appropriate social scientific concepts and vocabulary;
- be written in the author's own words;
- show an understanding of standard referencing conventions, although containing some errors and/or omissions.

A bare pass will meet some or many of the basic expectations of the assignment and is likely to:

- demonstrate basic skills in the areas identified in the 'clear pass' band;

but may also:

- answer the question tangentially;
- miss one (or more) key points;
- contain a number of inaccuracies or omissions;
- show only sparse coverage of relevant material;
- fail to support arguments with adequate evidence;
- be over-dependent on source material;
- contain only limited references.

A bare fail will not meet many of the basic expectations of the assignment and is likely to:

- fail to answer the question;
- contain limited appropriate material;

- show some evidence of relevant reading but provide only cursory coverage with a number of errors, omissions or irrelevances such that the writer's understanding of fundamental points is in question;
- be disorganized;
- contain much inappropriate material;
- lack any real argument or fail to support an argument with evidence;
- demonstrate a lack of understanding of social scientific concepts and vocabulary;
- demonstrate an inability to deploy social scientific writing skills such as skills of critical evaluation, synthesis, and so on;
- be unacceptably dependent on sources;
- include plagiarized material;
- demonstrate problems in the use of appropriate writing conventions such that the essay's meaning is frequently obscured;
- omit some or many references.

A clear or bad fail will meet few if any of the basic expectations of the assignment and is likely to:

- show a complete failure to understand or answer the question;
- show a profound misunderstanding of basic material;
- provide totally inadequate information;
- be incoherent;
- be plagiarized in whole or in part;
- omit references.

13.2 Writing skills: 'introductory', 'intermediate' and 'advanced' essays

As you move from entry level to more advanced undergraduate courses it is likely that you will be expected to develop and demonstrate an increasing range of essay-writing skills. For example, you may be expected to write from 'within' a particular perspective (see section 8.2), handle more complex theories, or systematically interrogate original sources (see section 5.1).

A general guide of this kind cannot give you a full breakdown of the skills that will be relevant to every course that you may take at every level. What it tries to do is provide an outline of 'core' skills. Individual courses may emphasize different parts of these core skills or may involve specific skills of their own (for example, project writing, employing specific research methods, using graphs to present information). Individual essays may also require you to emphasize some core skills more than others. As a result of these factors, you will need to adapt what is set out below according to the demands of different questions and different courses.

We look now in detail at the various criteria that distinguish 'basic' or success-ful 'introductory' undergraduate essays from 'intermediate' and 'advanced' essays.

The 'introductory' level essay

Introductions are likely to demonstrate:

- a clear understanding of the scope of the question and what is required;
- the ability to 'signpost' the shape of the essay's argument clearly and concisely;
- a basic ability to define key terms.

Main sections are likely to demonstrate some or all of the following, depending on what the question requires:

- an ability to construct a basic argument that engages with the question;
- the ability to précis aspects of relevant material clearly and concisely, often relying on commentaries and other secondary sources;
- the ability to outline, analyse and interpret evidence, arguments and the basics of relevant theories;
- the ability to support arguments with appropriate evidence and examples drawn from different sources;
- an ability to utilize basic maps, diagrams and numerical data in a way that supports the discussion;
- some familiarity with major perspectives in the social sciences;
- some familiarity with relevant social scientific vocabulary.

The main section of an introductory essay is also likely to be moving towards demonstrating:

- an understanding that different theories are in competition;
- the ability to outline the main similarities and differences between these;
- a basic ability to evaluate their strengths and weaknesses.

Conclusions are likely to demonstrate:

- the ability to summarize the content of the essay clearly and concisely and to come to a conclusion.

Quotations should be referenced, and 'pass' essays will always need to avoid plagiarism. Essays should 'flow' smoothly, use sentences, paragraphs and grammar correctly, and be written in clear English.

The 'intermediate' essay

In addition to skills in all the above areas, successful intermediate essays may also show the following.

Introductions are likely to demonstrate:

- a clear understanding of more complex essay questions;
- a basic ability to 'signpost' the content as well as the shape or structure of the essay, but not in a laboured way;
- a grasp of the major debates that lie 'behind the question';
- an ability to define key terms.

Main sections are likely to demonstrate some or all of the following, depending on what the question requires:

- the ability to construct more complex arguments relevant to the question;
- the ability to 'weight' different aspects of the material according to their significance within the overall argument;
- an ability to identify and précis the key debates relevant to the question;
- the ability to outline more complex theories in a basic form;
- an ability to relate abstract ideas and theories to concrete detail;
- an ability to support arguments with appropriate evidence and examples;
- an ability to utilize information drawn from across a wide range of source materials;
- the ability to evaluate critically – that is, identify the strengths and weaknesses of competing positions and make a reasoned choice between these;
- an ability to utilize more complex maps, diagrams and numerical data;
- a preliminary ability to work from original texts and data without relying on commentaries on these;
- increased familiarity with major social scientific perspectives and social scientific vocabulary, and increased confidence in applying these to specific issues;
- a preliminary ability to write from 'within' specific perspectives or theories;
- an ability to pull together different aspects of the course and apply these to the essay;
- an ability to select and use appropriate quotations from, and make references to, key texts in the field.

Conclusions are likely to demonstrate:

- the ability to highlight the essay's core argument;
- the ability to provide a basic summary of the key debates raised by the question and also provide an overview of the 'current state' of knowledge in the field;
- a preliminary ability to point to absences in the argument or areas worthy of future development.

Essays should also be properly referenced, be written in the author's own words, and utilize a more developed and fluent writing style (for example, by handling transitions effectively).

In four-year university undergraduate programmes, the successful shift from sophomore to junior intermediate work will often be indicated by a deeper understanding and more precise exposition on the course or module subjects, a stronger grasp of the academic field, and/or the ability to apply received knowledge to new case studies or novel examples.

The 'advanced' essay

In addition to skills in all of the above areas, successful advanced essays may also show the following.

Introductions are likely to demonstrate the ability:

- to present a more sophisticated or nuanced version of the essay's core argument;
- to summarize in more sophisticated forms the key debates raised by the question;
- to provide more sophisticated definitions of terms;
- to interrogate the question by focusing on ideas or sub-questions prompted by the question in hand.

Main sections are likely to demonstrate some or all of the following:

- the ability to construct complex arguments, 'weighting' each section according to its significance within the overall argument;
- the ability to provide sophisticated outlines of complex theories;
- the ability to support arguments with appropriate evidence and examples drawn from a wide range of sources, and to use evidence selectively in a way that supports central points;
- the ability to synthesize and evaluate competing positions critically and the confidence to write from 'within' a specific perspective or theory on the basis of a reasoned understanding of its strengths and weaknesses;
- where appropriate, recognition of the potential uncertainty, ambiguity and limits of knowledge in the field under discussion;
- familiarity with, and confidence in, handling complex maps, diagrams and numerical data;
- familiarity with, and confidence in, handling original texts and data without relying on commentaries;
- familiarity with the major social scientific perspectives and social scientific vocabulary, and confidence in applying these to specific issues and new contexts;
- the ability to pull together different aspects of the course and apply these to the issues raised by a specific essay question;
- the ability to use appropriate quotations and cite key texts in the field.

Conclusions are likely to demonstrate:

- the ability to present a sophisticated summary of the essay's core argument(s);
- the ability to provide an effective synthesis of the key debates raised by the question, alongside a sophisticated overview of the 'current state' of knowledge in the field;
- a developed ability to point to absences in the argument or areas worthy of future development.

'Advanced' essays should be fully referenced, citing a wide range of sources. The best essays are likely to show a significant depth of understanding of the issues raised by the question and may show a more creative or original approach (within the constraints of academic rigour).

Different skills, same writer

In thinking about the requirements of different levels of essay writing, it is important to realize that different levels of skills do not come neatly packaged. For instance, you may already possess advanced essay-writing skills even while working at an introductory level of undergraduate study. Alternatively, you may have advanced skills of analysis (such as the ability to break down a complex argument into its component parts and summarize these effectively), but struggle with handling theoretical concepts and perspectives. Or you may be very effective at your essay introductions, but shakier when it comes to ordering the argument in the main section. The important point to grasp is that the foregoing advice provides *indications* of what may be expected at different levels across the whole range of abilities, but it is *not* saying that you must be able to demonstrate the appropriate level of ability in all cases. Remember, too, that an essay is always greater than its component parts; it is how you put all those parts together that is often as important as the parts themselves.

You might like to look again at the Essays in Chapter 14. Can you identify some of the criteria above that led Essays 1 and 3 to receive higher marks, and Essays 2 and 4 to receive lower marks? On the basis of the criteria above, and what you have read elsewhere in this guide, are there clues as to whether the essays are written for beginning, intermediate or advanced courses? Are there other challenges you might set yourself as a reader or writer to check your understanding of the interplay between structure, content and style in deciding a grade for a particular essay?

Summary

- Essays are graded on the extent to which they demonstrate an understanding of relevant source material, and of social scientific and writing skills.
- The exact mix of content and skills required will depend on the course and question. However, it is possible to identify in general terms what is expected for each grade band.
- As you gain experience, you should expect your understanding of social scientific arguments and your writing skills to become increasingly sophisticated.

Self-test

1 What are some of the indicators of an excellent essay? How is this different at introductory and advanced levels of study?
2 What mistakes will you need to avoid if you want your essay to receive a 'pass' rather than a 'fail'?
3 For you personally, what are the potential problems that you can try to avoid when writing your next essay? What do you think are your particular strengths?

Don't forget! Visit **https://study.sagepub.com/redmanandmaples5** for more tasks and resources related to this chapter.

14

Examples of Student Essays

- Essay 1: 'School is a significant site in which sex/gender is produced.' Discuss. (2,000 words)
- Essay 2: 'School is a significant site in which sex/gender is produced.' Discuss. (2,000 words)
- Essay 3: Outline the argument that supermarkets constrain consumer choice. (1,250 words)
- Essay 4: Outline the argument that supermarkets constrain consumer choice. (1,250 words)

If you haven't already done so, read through the following examples of student essays. Essays 1 and 2 are written on the same topic; Essays 3 and 4 are written on another topic.

Essay 1 illustrates how applying the basic standards we have been discussing really can help to produce a good essay. It is a strong essay displaying more advanced writing skills. Depending on the exact requirements of the module, it would probably receive a grade at the top of the range. In contrast, Essay 2 is a weaker essay suggesting less developed social scientific writing skills. Although it would gain a pass mark, it would be at the lower end of the grade range. The word limit for Essays 1 and 2 is 2,000 words.

Essay 3, like Essay 1, is also a strong essay but one written for an introductory module. The Essay 3 question doesn't require the critical sophistication or nuance of Essay 1's, as you would expect from a lower-level module, but it does require an essay that makes clear links between social science claims and evidence. Essay 3 would receive a mark in the higher-grade bands, depending on the specific requirements of the module. You will see that

Essay 4 makes the crucial error of not answering the question. While some tutors would simply fail this essay, we think it is interesting and worth looking at for its merits (as well as its flaws). Given that the essay was written for an introductory social science course, Essay 4 could quite reasonably gain a pass mark, but towards the lower end of the grade bands. The word limit for Essays 3 and 4 is 1,250 words.

Essay 1

'School is a significant site in which sex/gender is produced.' Discuss.

This essay critically explores the claim that school is a significant site in which sex/gender is produced. The claim derives from a broadly social constructionist position, namely one that views sex/gender as being the product of social meanings and practices rather than something biologically given. The essay begins by outlining the social constructionist critique of the biological account of sex/gender. It then reviews recent research on gender and schooling to explore the extent to which the social meanings and practices that make up life in school may be seen as producing relational forms of masculinity and femininity. In exploring these issues, the essay endorses a broadly social constructionist standpoint on gender and schooling, although it also seeks to highlight a number of potential limitations to this position, particularly as these relate to the literature's account of the body and social agency.

Conventional or 'commonsense' accounts tend to view masculinity and femininity as biological categories characterized by a range of fixed physical and psychological differences in which the supposed attributes of masculinity (for example, rationality and the capacity for physical action) are valued over those of femininity (for example, intuition and the capacity for caring). The feminist cultural theorist Chris Weedon (1999) locates the origins of these ideas (at least in their contemporary form) in nineteenth-century biological theory and in Victorian middle-class values. However, she also points out that they have been reinvigorated in more recent work in the fields of sociobiology and evolutionary psychology (see for example, Thornhill and Palmer, 2000; Wilson, 1978).

The social constructionist position takes issue with this biologically reductive account. Drawing, in particular, on the work of Michel Foucault (1977, 1984), commentators from this perspective have sought to argue that masculinity and femininity cannot be understood as fixed biological categories but are instead produced in and through social meanings and practices. This position is distinct from earlier sociological accounts of 'sex role' (see, for example,

Rossi, 1985). Earlier accounts had tended to view gender as the social elaboration of an underlying biological sex difference. Social constructionist theory, on the other hand, argues that the notion of biological sex difference is itself a social construct. For example, Thomas Lacquer (1990) has demonstrated that the notion of distinct male and female bodies arose in the nineteenth century. Prior to this, maleness and femaleness were seen as variations on a single body. Equally, Judith Butler (1993, 2004) has argued that sex/gender is a 'performative enactment'. She suggests that, like other categories of the person, maleness and femaleness do not precede social meanings and practices but are brought into existence through an active 'gendering', that is the citation of sex/gender 'norms' embodied in what, following Foucault, she refers to as discursive practices. Importantly, Butler (1993, p. 238) also argues that gender is systematically (though not inevitably) produced through a 'heterosexual matrix' which equates 'proper forms of masculinity and femininity with heterosexuality and identifies gay masculinities and lesbian femininities as, in some way, "failed" or "damaged"'.

Bob Connell's influential work in the sociology of masculinity endorses this critique of biological essentialism but questions whether it risks writing the body out of existence. Connell suggests that forms of masculinity and femininity cannot be reduced to supposed biological differences but argues that bodies have 'forms of recalcitrance to social symbolism and control' (see, in particular, Connell, 1995, p. 56).

Connell also suggests that Butler's 'hard' social constructionist account risks writing social agency out of existence. Connell argues that there are multiple versions of masculinity (and, by implication, femininity) that are actively produced through relations of similarity to and difference from key social others. For example, forms of 'laddish', heterosexual, white working-class masculinity may be defined in opposition to forms of 'respectable' middle-class masculinity, to non-white ethnicities, to forms of femininity and to gay masculinities. This argument places a greater emphasis than does Butler's on the notion of pupils as 'active makers of their own sex/gender identities' (Mac an Ghaill, 1994, p. 90). Thus, whereas Butler tends to downplay agency (the active 'speaking' of sex/gender) in favour of a notion of performativity (being 'spoken by' social meanings and practices), Connell retains a stronger account of it.

Drawing on the work of the Italian Marxist Antonio Gramsci (1971), Connell also argues that masculinities and femininities can be understood as being engaged in 'hegemonic struggle'. This refers to an ongoing and potentially shifting process of competition, negotiation, alliance-building and sometimes coercion whereby, under particular conditions, particular versions of masculinity and femininity come to be 'culturally exalted' or 'idealized' while other versions are marginalized and subordinated (see Connell, 1990, p. 83).

Broadly social constructionist ideas of this kind have informed a body of recent literature on sex/gender and schooling (see for example, Duncan, 1999; Epstein and Johnson, 1998; Kehily, 2002; Mac an Ghaill, 1994; Martino and Meyenn, 2001; Martino and Pallotta-Chiarolli, 2003; Skelton and Francis, 2003; Thorne, 1993).

Within this literature, schools are seen as significant sites in which sex/gender is actively produced. This is to say that sex/gender is viewed not as something that is simply brought into the school ready formed but as something actively produced and reproduced in the processes and practices of schooling itself. This active production of sex/gender has a number of dimensions and the following discussion focuses on three of these: the ways in which the content and practices of schooling encode sex/gender; the ways in which pupils actively use sex/gender to negotiate schooling; and the ways in which sex/gender intersects with other social relations.

Perhaps the most obvious means by which sex/gender is said to be produced in the social constructionist literature is via the content and practices of schooling itself. For example, Thorne's (1993) study of two US elementary schools draws attention to the ways in which the categorization of children by gender is threaded through the material and social fabric of the school, such as in teachers' talk ('There's three girls need to get busy', p. 34) or the organization and management of learning (for instance, dividing pupils into gender-based 'teams', p. 67). Similarly, Epstein and Johnson (1994, p. 214) point to the ways in which the regulation of pupils' clothing (in particular, sanctions against girls' clothing thought to connote too overt a sexuality) frequently embodies notions of 'appropriate' or 'proper' forms of gender. While Thorne (1993, pp. 35–6) draws attention to the fact that many aspects of schooling will also play down or contradict gender categorizations, it remains the case that the content and practices of schooling encode sex/gender as a significant category of difference.

However, while sex/gender can be said to be encoded in the content and practices of schooling, the literature also suggests that pupils are themselves active agents in its production. Thorne (1993), for example, describes the children in her study as engaging in 'borderwork', practices by which they actively produce, strengthen and assert sex/gender differences. For instance, she describes a game of team handball which began as a co-operative and informal activity in which gender was not strongly marked but which rapidly accelerated into a more aggressive interaction themed as 'the boys against the girls' (p. 65). In this moment, Thorne suggests, sex/gender was being actively produced (or in Butler's terms, 'performatively enacted') as a significant category of difference.

As well as producing sex/gender through friendship group interactions, the literature also suggests that pupils use sex/gender to negotiate and resist schooling. Kehily and Nayak (1996, p. 214) describe an account from a group of secondary school pupils in which one of them (Samantha) was claimed to have pursued a teacher (Mr Smedley) round the classroom with a sprig of mistletoe with the intention of 'getting some lipstick on the top of his head'. In this instance, a heterosexualized form of femininity is used satirically to undermine the authority of a male teacher (see also Walkerdine, 1981).

While heterosexualized forms of sex/gender are clearly deployed to subvert adult authority, it is also possible to argue that sex/gender is used to negotiate schooling in more subtle ways. For instance, Connell has argued that boys use masculinity to negotiate or build a 'subjective orientation' to the curriculum and that, in the process, the curriculum is important in producing differentiated forms of masculinity. He writes:

> the differentiation of masculinities occurs in relation to a school curriculum that organizes knowledge hierarchically, and sorts students into an academic hierarchy. By institutionalizing academic failure via competitive grading and streaming, the school forces differentiation on the boys. ... Social power in terms of access to higher education, entry to professions, command of communication, is being delivered by the school system to boys who are academic 'successes'. The reaction of the 'failed' is likely to be a claim to other sources of power, even other definitions of masculinity. Sporting prowess, physical aggression, sexual conquest, may do. (Connell, 1993, p. 95)

This general argument informs Máirtín Mac an Ghaill's (1994) study of a multi-ethnic English secondary school. Mac an Ghaill identifies a variety of differentiated masculinities – the 'macho lads', the 'academic achievers', the 'new enterprisers', and the 'real Englishmen' – through which boys in the school collectively negotiated the curriculum, their home backgrounds and their perceived employment futures. The 'new enterprisers' were, perhaps, particularly interesting in that they broke with the conventional distinction (identified by Connell, above) between anti-academic, 'laddish' forms of masculinity, and pro-school masculinities validated by academic success. Mac an Ghaill argues that the 'new enterprisers' were able to build a pro-school masculine identification out of a newly vocationalized curriculum that offered recognition for academic success in non-traditional subject areas, especially Information and Communication Technologies.

The final area highlighted by the social constructionist literature as a means by which sex/gender is produced in the school concerns the ways in which masculinities and femininities are produced in and through relations of similarity to and difference from social others. As discussed above, Thorne's (1993) concept of 'borderwork' draws our attention to the ways in which sex/gender is used by pupils to produce themselves in gender-differentiated terms. This opposition between forms of masculinity and femininity is perhaps the most central relation underpinning pupils' sex/gender identifications in the school. However, both Mac an Ghaill (1994) and Epstein and Johnson (1998) underline the extent to which school-based masculinities and femininities are also produced in and through relations of age, class, ethnicity and sexuality, as well as in relation to forms of masculinity and femininity deemed subordinate or otherwise inferior.

For instance, Epstein and Johnson cite an exchange between a group of four Muslim girls in a large single-sex comprehensive in which a fifth girl is described in the following terms:

> Shamira is not traditional [i.e. she does not occupy a conservative form of Muslim ethnicity]. She is a big tart and wears lipstick that doesn't suit her and she walks around sticking her tits out (Epstein and Johnson, 1998, p. 117).

The girls in this example can be seen to be constructing their own femininity in opposition to Shamira, whose femininity is deemed inappropriately westernized and sexualized. This, then, is an example where sex/gender is spoken through intra-ethnic identifications (traditional versus westernized) and through an opposition to a subordinated femininity (the 'madonna' versus the 'whore'). As Epstein and Johnson also argue, although drawing on wider social relations, such gender constructions occur within and are specific to the dynamics of individual schools.

The girls' appraisal of Shamira in terms of sexuality underlines the centrality of sex and sexuality to the production and policing of gender in pupils' cultures. Mac an Ghaill (1994, pp. 90–6), for instance, describes the ways in which the secondary school boys in his study worked at producing masculinity through 'competitive and compulsive' sexualized talk and practice within their friendship groups. This consisted of the sexual-objectification of girls and women and the homophobic harassment of boys perceived as gay or 'insufficiently masculine'. Epstein and Johnson (1998, p. 158) suggest that anti-lesbian harassment appears less central to girls' culture than does anti-gay harassment to boys' culture. Nevertheless, as the Shamira example demonstrates, they argue that heterosexualized appraisal of other girls is central to the production of femininity within girls' friendship groups.

The recent social constructionist literature has, therefore, made a systematic case in support of the proposition that schooling is a significant site in which sex/gender is produced. It argues that the content and practices of schooling encode sex/gender; that pupils actively use gender to negotiate schooling; and that gender is produced within local pupils' cultures through relations of similarity to and difference from key social others. Work on the relationship between gender and sexuality in the context of the school has been particularly significant. Such arguments, I would argue, fundamentally undermine biologically determinist readings of sex/gender. Nevertheless, it may be possible to qualify the social constructionist account. In particular, following Connell, it is possible to argue that the theoretical tension between a 'hard' social constructionist account (in which social agency is replaced by a notion of performativity) and the emphasis in the literature on pupils as 'active makers of sex gender identities' is not fully addressed or resolved. Equally, it may also be possible to argue that the literature does not fully resolve the exact status of the body in the social constructionist account. However, it remains the case that the recent literature on gender and schooling significantly adds to our understanding of the social construction of gender and sexuality.

Word Count: 2,228

References

Butler, J. (1993) *Bodies That Matter*, London, Routledge.
Butler, J. (2004) *Undoing Gender*, London, Routledge.
Connell, R.W. (1990) 'An iron man: the body and some contradictions of hegemonic masculinity', in Messner, M.A. and Sabo, D.F. (eds), *Sport, Men and the Gender Order: Critical Feminist Perspectives*, Champaign, IL, Human Kinetics.
Connell, R.W. (1993) 'Cool guys, swots and wimps: the interplay of masculinity and education', in Angus, L. (ed.), *Education, Inequality and Social Identity*, London, Falmer Press.
Connell, R.W. (1995) *Masculinities*, Cambridge, Polity Press.
Duncan, N. (1999) *Sexual Bullying: Gender Conflict and Pupil Culture in Secondary Schools*, London: Routledge.
Epstein, D. and Johnson, R. (1994) 'On the straight and the narrow: the heterosexual presumption, homophobias and schools', in Epstein, D. (ed.), *Challenging Lesbian and Gay Inequalities in Education*, Buckingham, Open University Press.
Epstein, D. and Johnson, R. (1998) *Schooling Sexualities*, Buckingham, Open University Press.
Foucault, M. (1977) *Discipline and Punish: The Birth of the Prison*, Harmondsworth, Penguin.
Foucault, M. (1984) *The History of Sexuality, Vol. 1: An Introduction*, Harmondsworth, Penguin/Peregrine.
Gramsci, A. (1971) *Selections from the Prison Notebooks*, London, Lawrence and Wishart.
Kehily, M.J. (2002) *Sexuality, Gender and Schooling: Shifting Agendas in Social Learning*, London, Routledge.
Kehily, M.J. and Nayak, A. (1996) 'The Christmas kiss: sexuality, storytelling and schooling', *Curriculum Studies*, vol. 4, no. 2, pp. 211–28.
Lacquer, T.W. (1990) *Making Sex: Body and Gender from the Greeks to Freud*, Cambridge, MA, Harvard University Press.

Mac an Ghaill, M. (1994) *The Making of Men: Masculinities, Sexualities and Schooling*, Buckingham, Open University Press.

Martino, W. and Meyenn, B. (eds) (2001) *What About the Boys? Issues of Masculinity in Schools*, Buckingham, Open University Press.

Martino, W. and Pallotta-Chiarolli, M. (eds) (2003) *So What's a Boy? Addressing Issues of Masculinity and Schooling*, Buckingham, Open University Press.

Rossi, A.S. (1985) 'Gender and parenthood', in Rossi, A.S. (ed.), *Gender and the Life Course*, New York, Aldine.

Skelton, C. and Francis, B. (eds) (2003) *Boys and Girls in the Primary Classroom*, Buckingham: Open University Press.

Thorne, B. (1993) *Gender Play: Girls and Boys in School*, Buckingham, Open University Press.

Thornhill, R. and Palmer, C.T. (2000) *A Natural History of Rape: Biological Bases of Sexual Coercion*, Cambridge, MA, MIT Press.

Walkerdine, V. (1981) 'Sex, power and pedagogy', *Screen Education*, no. 38, pp. 14–24.

Weedon, C. (1999) *Feminism, Theory and the Politics of Difference*, Oxford, Blackwell.

Wilson, E.O. (1978) *On Human Nature*, Cambridge, MA, Harvard University Press.

Commentary on Essay 1

In reviewing this essay we are not particularly concerned as to whether the answer is 'right' or not. The literature it draws on is from cultural studies and sociology and it is undoubtedly the case that the question of sex/gender could have been addressed from a number of alternative disciplinary points of view – for example, developmental psychology or biology – that might have generated different arguments. Instead, the issue of interest to us is the extent to which the answer demonstrates effective social scientific writing skills. As with any piece of work, the essay is not without flaws. For instance, it could be argued that evidence in support of the 'conventional' view of gender is not explored systematically enough to be rejected with such certainty by the author (although this may simply reflect the balance of argument in the literature the author was required to read). Equally, it could be argued that the concept of sex/gender 'performativity' is not fully explained and that it is not fully illustrated through the research evidence cited. Similarly, the critique of the literature on schooling and sex/gender in the conclusion (the arguments about the status of the body and social agency) appears to repeat Connell's theoretical points without really growing out of the evidence explored in the main section of the essay.

Having said this, the essay has a number of strengths that suggest it should receive a grade towards the top end of the range. Let's explore these in terms of structure and writing skills, content and social scientific skills.

Structure and writing skills

- The essay begins with an introduction that identifies the subject of the essay, indicates the debate lying 'behind' the question, signposts its content and establishes the author's position. (See sections 7.1 and 8.4.)
- The main section uses a standard 'evaluative' structure, that is, it outlines competing positions then explores the evidence for and against them before coming to a conclusion. (See section 4.3.)
- It builds a logically progressing argument that develops through the following steps: the social constructionist argument is more convincing than the conventional biological account; this is because sex/gender is 'performative' and relational; this can be demonstrated in relation to schooling. (See section 8.1.)
- It 'flows' reasonably smoothly, is well signposted (see section 8.4) throughout (for instance, paragraphs 1 and 7), makes use of summary/introductory points (for example, in the statement, 'As well as producing sex/gender through friendship group interactions, the literature also suggests that … '), and makes accurate use of spelling, grammar, paragraphing and sentence structure. (See section 8.4.)
- It provides an evaluative conclusion that summarizes the preceding argument, provides a clear endorsement of the statement in the question, and identifies potential absences in the argument. (See Chapter 9.)
- It is slightly long (2,228 words) but is probably just on the outer limits of acceptability. (As with other regulations, remember to check the rules on essay length that apply to the actual course you are studying.) (See section 2.3.)

Content

Effective coverage of theoretical issues and research evidence is clearly central to any essay answer. The author of this essay appears to have used or referenced a range of relevant sources and provided detailed coverage of both theoretical material and research evidence. Without knowing the exact content of the course she or he was studying it is difficult to comment on this in much detail, but the coverage looks thorough and the detailed handling of the material suggests wide-ranging reading and a good understanding of the issues.

Social scientific skills

- The answer addresses the question set. (See sections 2.3 and 4.2.)
- The essay is effectively referenced, including page details where necessary. (See Chapter 10.)
- It makes good use of relevant quotations. The Connell quotation is a 'classic' statement of the social constructionist position. The quotation from Epstein and Johnson adds some 'colour' to the argument and is effective in illustrating and illuminating a complex argument. Both support rather than replace points made by the author. (See section 8.3.)

- Within the confines of a 2,000-word essay, it provides a complex and thorough engagement with relevant theory and applies this theory to and supports it with empirical evidence. (See sections 2.2 and 8.2.)
- The essay demonstrates effective skills of selection and summary. (See sections 3.3 and 8.2.)
- It provides an effective evaluation of relevant concepts, debates and evidence. (See sections 2.2, 4.2 and 8.2.)
- It comes to a clear conclusion that is supported by the preceding argument. (See Chapter 9.)
- It makes good use of appropriate academic vocabulary and concepts. (See sections 8.2 and 8.4.)

Now let's take a look at Essay 2.

Essay 2

'School is a significant site in which sex/gender is produced.' Discuss.

This essay looks at the arguments for and against the idea that school is a significant site in which gender is produced. The first section shows where this idea comes from and contrasts it to the deterministic account. The second section gives evidence in favour of the theory of Social Constructionism.

We are used to thinking that gender is biological. Men are men and women are women and this is natural. Sociobiologists and evolutionary psychologists would agree with this point of view. This is called 'Deterministic'. Men are better at rational tasks and thinking in three dimensions. They are also stronger. Women are better at intuition thinking and emotionality. E.O. Wilson is an example of this approach. However, writers such as Foucolt, Butler and Connell have challenged this. They argue that gender is constructed in practices and meanings, such as the 'enactment of gender norms'. Butler calls this 'performativity'.

Connell argues that gender is hegemonic'. This means that there are different types of masculinity in competition but that certain types (such as sportsmen) are 'idealized' (Connell, 1990). Connell got this idea from Gramsci, an Italian Marxist. An example of hegemonic masculinity is given by Swain who argues that playing football in the playground makes boys dominant in the school because this draws on a sporting version of masculinity that is dominant in the wider society (Swain, 2000).

Foucolt is very important in this Social Constructionist theory. He argued that the term 'homosexual' does not refer to a pre-existing identity but constructs that identity. This does not mean that same-sex sexual activity did not happen before the nineteenth century (when the term homosexual was invented), it means that that same-sex sexual activity did not imply a particular type of personality (the homosexual) before this. The homosexual is therefore Socially Constructed as of course is the heterosexual. Butler argues that biological sex is also a Social Construction (Butler, 1993).

Schools are a place where Social Construction happens. This has been argued by many eminent Academic thinkers including Mac an Ghaill and Epstein. Connell argues that masculinities appear in relation to the curriculum.

> the differentiation of masculinities occurs in relation to a school curriculum that organizes knowledge hierarchically, and sorts students into an academic hierarchy. By institutionalizing academic failure via competitive grading and streaming, the school forces differentiation on the boys ... Social power in terms of access to higher education, entry to professions, command of communication, is being delivered by the school system to boys who are academic 'successes'. The reaction of the 'failed' is likely to be a claim to other sources of power, even other definitions of masculinity. Sporting prowess, physical aggression, sexual conquest, may do. (Connell, 1993)

This is one way that schools Socially Construct gender.

A second way is that children actively produce gender for themselves. Take the example of children lining up to leave the classroom. They used to be told to form lines so that girls were in one line and boys were in another. In fact, I remember that in my first school it still had two entrances one marked for boys and the other for girls. Foucolt would see this as an example of the ways in which schools produce sexual difference. Now however girls and boys will be told to form a single line but Barry Thorne argues they will still try to form lines according to gender.

This is an example of boys and girls actively producing gender for themselves which Thorn calls 'borderwork' (Thorn, 1993).

Sexuality is a big theme in much of this writing on schooling and gender. There are lots of examples where children use sexuality to try to undermine there teachers. A famous one is Valerie Walkerdines example of two little boys calling their nursery teacher rude names. Many people are surprised that children as young as this would dare to be so cheeky. Another example is the 'Christmas kiss' story told by Kehily and Nayak (1996). In this case a secondary school girl chased her male teacher round the classroom with a sprig of mistletoe and claimed she was trying to kiss him on the head. The pupils liked to retell this story so that the story itself was one way in which they 'had a laff' and resisted the authority of the school. Unfortunately the teacher had a nervous breakdown. These examples also show how gender is used in the classroom to 'negotiate the curriculum' indicating how schools Socially Construct gender.

Mac an Ghaill (1994) is very interested in the ways in which boys use homophobic abuse to police other boys. To be identified as a sissy is to invite homophobic abuse whether or not on defines oneself as gay, often in the form of more or less ritualized humour. The use of humour and insult constitutes a regulatory practice by young men in schools through which they establish and exhibit heterosexual masculinities. The forms humour and insult employed are primarily either sexist (for example, the teasing and harassment of girls or insult to other boys via insulting their mothers or sisters) or homophobic abuse of young men who did not display 'hyper-masculinity'. Swain talks about this too. He describes how the football-playing boys in his research would abuse boys who weren't very good at football by calling them 'Gaylord' and 'poofter'. Since these boys were at primary school calling them homosexual was not because they were homosexual but because this was a way of saying they were like girls. The point Swain is making is that football is a dominant form of masculinity in our society and that the boys in the school tried to lay claim to dominance in there own right by being good at football. However, this dominance was also at the expense of other social groups such as girls, homosexuality and boys who weren't any good at football. Mac an Ghaill argues that boys 'make up' collective identities as boys out of a Compulsory Heterosexuality, Misogyny and Homophobia.

> heterosexual male students were involved in a double relationship, of traducing the 'other', including women and gays (external relations), at the same time as expelling femininity and homosexuality from within themselves (internal relations). (Man an Ghaill, p. 90)

Barry Thorne describes how one boy in her research was called a 'sissy' by other boys because he wore a one-piece snow suit which they thought was 'wimpy' and because he liked to play girl's games in the playground as well as playing boys games. She says he was a bit of a loner and didn't have many friends. Some children were more likely to get away with this sort of thing. A girl got away with it because she was a good athlete and because she could fight which gave her respect with the other children. But one of the teachers described her as 'wanting to be a boy'.

There are three ways that schools produce gender. The pupils produce gender for themselves. The school produces gender through things like making children line up in different lines. And the children 'negotiate the curriculum'.

In conclusion, this has essay has presented a lot of evidence to show that 'school is a significant site in which gender is produced'. In fact, Christine Heward describes schools as 'masculinity factories' and I would tend to agree with her. Gender is obviously very important in the school day. Schools are always doing things that reproduce gender even though they sometimes try to do the opposite of this. And even when schools do try do the opposite of this the children themselves resist this by reproducing conventional ideas about gender (Thorne). Butler calls this 'performativity' but you could see it from the 'Deterministic' point of view of which EO Wilson is an example which would argue that the children are just being boys and girls because they are programmed to be this way by Evolution. This argument is difficult to get away from at the end of the day because there are some obvious differences between men and women so we probably should expect to see these in children as well. I would argue that we need to have a Middle Ground where we put together the Deterministic and the Social Constructionist point of views. In fact, this is what Connell argues when he says that you cant get away from the body.

The body, I would conclude is inescapable (Connell).

Word Count: 1401

References

Butler, J. (1993) 'Bodies That Matter'.

Connell, R.W. (1995) *Masculinities*, Polity Press.

Epstein, D. and Johnson, R. (1998) *Schooling Sexualities*, Buckingham: Open University Press.

Foucault (1977) *Discipline and Punish: The Birth of the Prison*,

Kehily, M.J. and Nayak, A. (1996) '*The Christmas kiss: Sexuality, storytelling and schooling*', Curriculum Studies.

Mac an Ghaill, M. (1994) 'The Making of Men: Masculinities, Sexualities and Schooling', Buckingham: Open University Press.

Swain, J. (2000) 'The money's good, the fame's good, the girls are good: the role of playground football in the construction of young boys' masculinity in a junior school', *British Journal of Sociology of Education*, 21, 1: 95–109.

Commentary on Essay 2

You can probably see for yourself that this essay is not as strong an answer to the question as that provided by Essay 1. Why is this? Again, we can break down our thoughts into issues related to structure and writing skills, content and social scientific skills.

Structure and writing skills

Although the essay has an introduction, conclusion and some signposting, its structure and the writing skills displayed are weak. In particular:

- The introduction is underdeveloped compared to Essay 1. It does not establish the author's position on the question and both the signposting (see section 8.4) and the allusion to the debate lying 'behind' the question are vague. (See section 7.1.)
- There are systematic errors in spelling and punctuation (e.g. 'there' instead of 'their'; incorrect use of the apostrophe; unnecessary use of capital letters on terms such as 'social constructionism'); sentences are sometimes cumbersome (see section 8.4) and paragraphs are sometimes too short. (See section 12.4.)
- There are errors in the spelling of several authors' names (Foucolt instead of Foucault; Barry Thorne instead of Barrie Thorne).
- The brief section beginning, 'To be identified as a sissy is to invite homophobic abuse … ', and ending, 'homophobic abuse of young men who did not display "hyper-masculinity"', is plagiarized from Epstein and Johnson (1998, p. 181). (See section 12.5.)
- Although the essay begins by discussing theory and then moves on to look at empirical evidence, the logical progression of the argument is problematic. For instance, the relevance of paragraph 5 to the question needs to be more clearly established, while the material on sexuality and schooling is not clearly located as an example of the ways in which gender is produced in schooling practices. (See sections 6.2 and 8.1.)
- Given the word limit (2,000), the essay is rather short (1,401 words). (See section 12.1.) (Remember to check the rules on essay length that apply to the actual course you are studying.)

Content

The material covered appears to be relevant to the question set, drawing on similar literature to Essay 1. However, the understanding of this material appears to be much shallower in comparison to that displayed in Essay 1 and the breadth of detailed reading (as evidenced in the identification of major arguments and relevant evidence) appears more limited.

Social scientific skills

Once again, these areas are weak compared to Essay 1.

- Referencing is inconsistent and incomplete. (See Chapter 10.)
- The introduction and conclusion are thin. (See Chapters 7 and 9.)
- Handling of theory is poor, suggesting an inadequate understanding of the material. For example, although the discussion of Foucault and homosexuality is good, the concepts of performativity and hegemony are not fully explained. (See sections 2.2 and 8.3.)
- Both the Mac an Ghaill quotation and the first Connell quotation are used without a full explanation of the points being made. (See sections 6.2 and 8.3.)
- The empirical evidence is sometimes left to 'speak for itself' without a full explanation of the point it is being used to illustrate or support. (See section 8.2.)

- The information cited about the author's own schooldays detracts from the professionalism of the argument by appearing merely anecdotal. (See section 12.3.)
- The evaluative conclusion is undermined by an incorrect understanding of Connell's argument about the relationship between the body and the social.
- Use of appropriate academic vocabulary is underdeveloped. (See section 8.2.)

Essays 3 and 4 address a different question but again demonstrate the ways in which good academic practice can produce a stronger essay.

Essay 3

Outline the argument that supermarket power constrains consumer choice.

In this essay I will outline the argument that supermarket power, despite appearing to promote consumer choice, actually constrains it. Supermarket power can be described as '... the ability of supermarkets to flex their economic muscle' (Allen and Blakeley, 2014, p. 157) and '... to act in the marketplace in ways that their rivals can do little or nothing about' (p. 154). However, there are also other ways in which supermarkets can exert power, and these will be examined throughout the essay.

Zygmunt Bauman claims we have shifted from an industrial society to a consumer one, whereby the idea of consumer freedom dominates, and lives are shaped more and more by what appears to be an abundant marketplace. He argues that '[c]onsumption is a key means for establishing and maintaining status within society' (cited in Allen and Blakeley, 2014, p. 129). In other words, consumption is not only about buying what you need; purchasing certain items can be 'visibly displaying status to others' (Allen and Blakeley, 2014, p. 133) and this desire to display can influence what we buy. Ernest Dichter was a psychologist who argued that possessions were 'an extension of [individuals] ... and their personalities' (cited in Allen and Blakeley, 2014, p. 197): he understood that advertisers could exploit this to encourage the purchase of certain brands. In a society where consumption is linked with portrayal of an image to others, and products become an expression or extension of the self, according to Allen and Blakeley, supermarkets can actively use their advertising power to 'tap into the unconscious desires and emotional needs of consumers' (p. 196). Whether consciously or unconsciously, we are enticed to a particular projected self-image or lifestyle by brands and products which play on emotions and make us desire them. Certainly 'the promotion of needs and the projection of desires act as pressures for individuals and groups to conform to accepted ways of consuming' (p. 143). The advertising power of supermarkets can therefore be seen to shape consumer choice.

Supermarkets wield power in other ways. One way in which super-markets exert market power is through bargaining down prices from food wholesalers, manufacturers and subcontractors, due to their ability to buy in greater volumes and therefore 'extract more favourable terms ... [or] demand discounts, [whether] from a small dairy farmer or T-shirt manufacturer' (Allen and Blakeley, 2014, p. 155). This clearly has an impact on smaller businesses who buy in smaller volumes and are there-fore unable to bargain with wholesalers in the same way as the global supermarket chains. Worse, however, is when supermarkets sell goods below cost as a strategy for cornering the local market. Even where there are objections to this sort of anti-competitive practice, supermarkets can 'use their size and influence to ... brush community opinion aside' (Allen and Blakeley, 2014, p. 155) and press on with practices that may lead to the closure of smaller shops.

Supermarkets are also in a very strong position when dealing with local planners and government bodies, which can restrict further the voice of consumers such as those lobbying against more supermarkets being opened (or expanded) in their areas. A 2011 survey of small and medium-sized grocers 'identified the main obstacle to their business as competition from the big supermarket chains' (Allen and Blakeley, 2014, p. 163). Concern about supermarkets from smaller grocery stores is understand-able. According to Helena Rimmer of Friends of the Earth there is evidence of a 30–40% decrease in local shops where a Tesco Express has opened (The Open University, 2015). Rimmer argues that there is no 'real choice' for consumers if they are simply choosing between, for instance, Tesco's and Sainsbury's. Real choice, she says, would include a variety of retailers, including street markets, butchers and other small businesses. Allen and Blakeley note that those who wish to 'make purchases on an ethical basis or in smaller, more local shops than Tesco' are also restricted if these shops have been forced into closure by the powerful supermarkets (2014, p. 49). Perhaps unsurprisingly, there are, Rimmer says, over 200 communities lobbying against development plans for supermarkets (The Open University, 2015).

Supermarkets opening in the high street may reduce the number of local shops, thus reducing consumer choice, but supermarket power can also cre-ate consumer inequalities. Where supermarkets set up in out of town locations, not only does this impact on the high street, it can create prob-lems of accessibility for those who, for example, do not own cars, or suffer from a disability which makes it difficult to travel, as well as for others. Bauman uses the terms 'seduced' and 'repressed' to represent different types of consumer and the inequalities between them. According to Bauman, the seduced can actively 'consume' and participate effectively in a consumer society, as they have the means to do so. The repressed, however, are, 'excluded from this consumer society or ... pushed to its margins ...' (Allen and Blakeley, 2014, p. 127). The repressed have limited 'life chances' in that they cannot consume in a way that is necessary or desired. The unemployed, those who receive low wages, or newly arrived migrants could all be part of the 'repressed' group. Linking this to the power of supermarkets, it could be argued that the closures of smaller, local 'high street' shops are narrowing the choices of the repressed further, in terms of variety of retailer, variance in price, location, and the creation of potential issues around accessibility.

Anti-supermarket campaigners argue that there are also wider, global social and economic impacts that arise from the dominance of supermarkets. Their 'stranglehold over the food and clothing supply chain' (Allen and Blakeley, 2014, p. 157) creates risks for suppliers and producers, which consumers effectively, though perhaps unwittingly, support by doing their shopping at the supermarket. Workers in the UK and abroad, including child workers, are subject to low pay and sometimes seriously unsafe working conditions, due to the supermarkets' interest in driving down costs. The impact and 'real price' of low cost goods that supermarkets provide can be measured in lives, as for instance in the 2013 Rana Plaza fire where 1,100 workers died due to poor safety conditions (Open University, 2014).

In summary, supermarkets influence consumer choice in a number of ways. According to Bauman, Dichter and Allen and Blakeley, consumer behaviour is shaped by advertising, and supermarkets have large advertising budgets with which to entice consumers. By exerting their bargaining power with wholesalers, global supermarket chains are able to price goods lower than smaller, local companies are able to, further enticing consumers. High street supermarkets' lower prices drive out competition, and lead to the closure of other local, high street shops. Locating supermarkets out of town has similar effects on local high street shops, but can also create issues in relation to accessibility for consumers, further limiting choice for Bauman's 'repressed' group. Furthermore, supermarkets' influence over local planners and politicians can mean they are able to ignore community protests about supermarket developments. Supermarkets also limit consumer choice around ethical issues such as working conditions and low wages for workers in the UK and abroad. While supermarkets appear to offer abundance for consumers, the issues explored here instead suggest that in significant ways supermarket power actually constrains consumer choice.

Word count: 1,203

Reference List

Staples, M. (2014) 'Making Lives' in Allen, J. and Blakeley, G. (eds) *Understanding Social Lives, Part 1*, Milton Keynes, The Open University.

Havard, C. and Hetherington, K. (2014) 'Consumer society? Identity and Lifestyle', in Allen, J. and Blakeley, G. (eds) *Understanding Social Lives, Part 1*, Milton Keynes, The Open University.

Allen, J. (2014) 'Supermarket power: winners and losers', in Allen, J. and Blakeley, G. (eds) *Understanding Social Lives, Part 1*, Milton Keynes, The Open University.

Havard, C. and Revill, G. (2014) 'Advertising and consumer choice: the powers of persuasion', in Allen, J. and Blakeley, G. (eds) *Understanding Social Lives, Part 1*, Milton Keynes, The Open University.

The Open University (2015) *'Evidence in the social sciences'* [Audio], *DD102 Introducing the Social Sciences*. Available at https://learn2.open.ac.uk/mod/oucontent/view.php?id=698890&section=3.2

The Open University (2015) *'Reflecting on 'Making Lives''* [Audio], *DD102 Introducing the Social Sciences*. Available at https://learn2.open.ac.uk/mod/oucontent/view.php?id=698897&section=4

The Open University (2015) 'Inequalities on the street' [Video], *DD102 Introducing the Social Sciences*. Available at https://learn2.open.ac.uk/mod/oucontent/view.php?id=698875&section=2.2 (Accessed 21 October 2015).

Commentary on Essay 3

The topic of Essays 3 and 4 is the power of supermarkets over consumer choice, but the assignment is also an exercise in using social science tools, in this case outlining claims, and using evidence to support those claims.

Essay 3 correctly addresses the essay requirement, with a regular essay structure of introduction, main body and conclusion, covering a number of important claims about supermarket power, and backing up those claims with evidence. While there are flaws, you will probably recognise that Essay 3 has many of the features of a strong social science essay. What makes this introductory level essay particularly striking, however, is that the student shows evidence of *thinking* like a social scientist (you can make out the stages of the circuit of knowledge being worked through the essay).

Structure and writing skills

- The introduction begins with a 'foil' for the main argument; noting that contrary to conventional wisdom, supermarkets don't offer consumers 'abundance'. It then proceeds with a definition of supermarket power, in the form of two short quotations. Using quotations in the introduction is generally not considered good practice in social science essay writing. In fact, despite being an interesting start to the essay, the introduction fails to do its main job, which is to tell the reader, clearly, what the essay is about, and signpost its key features (see Chapter 7). The final sentence about the 'other ways' supermarkets exert power is too vague for the reader to get a good sense of the specific content of the essay. However, we do learn that supermarket power isn't only about economic power and the marketplace, and this leads us into the first main paragraph.

- The main section is effectively a list of some of the claims about supermarket power, fleshed out with examples and quotations (see section 8.2 and 8.3), which is perfectly appropriate for this sort of essay, at this level. (See sections 4.2, 4.3 and 12.2.)
- Some of the claims are more nuanced than others, perhaps most particularly in the first main section paragraph, where the author shows real skill in explaining the connection between a consumer society, advertising and how these shape consumer behaviour and therefore choice. (See sections 2.2, 3.3 and 6.1.) There are, however, far too many quotations in one paragraph. (See section 8.3.) Remember that quotations should be used sparingly. There is no hard and fast rule about the number of quotations in a paragraph, but one is plenty and three is probably too many.
- The second paragraph marks a shift in focus to a claim about supermarket size and buying power, and this is nicely signposted. (See section 8.4.) Arguably, there are too many thoughts crammed into one paragraph – however, the argument flows and the broad claim of supermarket size being an advantage holds the different examples together. (See sections 8.1 and 8.4.)
- The theme of supermarkets' wider influence is developed in the third paragraph which makes excellent use of statistics as evidence to support two related claims. (See section 8.2.) Notice also how the author begins this paragraph with a note about 'the voice of consumers' and brings us back to the idea of this voice in the final sentence about the number of petitions against supermarket developments. (See section 8.4.)
- The fourth paragraph considers consumer inequalities, and introduces Bauman's concepts, 'seduced' and 'repressed', which are tidily defined. (See section 2.2.) Arguably, this paragraph has more in common with the first main paragraph than it does with the ones that precede or follow it, so there could be a case for re-organizing the essay a bit. That said, this is a strong paragraph that succinctly outlines consumer inequality issues. (See section 4.2.)
- The final main section paragraph feels a bit like an add-on structurally, as it is more about working conditions than the relationship between supermarket power and consumer choice. However, the author has done an admirable job of connecting unsafe working conditions to supermarkets driving down production costs – and to the argument that consumers, through their supermarket purchases, effectively support this (an unwitting 'choice'). (See sections 2.2 and 6.1.)
- The conclusion does its job: it accurately summarizes the essay's content, by restating the main claims of each paragraph (see Chapter 9), but in a slightly different order. It then returns to the starting point 'foil', and concludes with a clear statement about supermarket power and consumer choice.
- The writing throughout is clear, with good word choice, good–excellent sentence construction, and sentences being built into, sometimes excellent, coherent paragraphs. (See sections 8.1, 8.4 and 12.5.)

- The word count, set at 1,250 words, is within a 10 per cent allowance. (See section 2.3.)
- The spelling, grammar and punctuation are generally all good. (See section 12.4.)
- The logic of the essay is good and the flow is okay: the essay question invites an outline which we would expect to cover a range of points or claims. (See section 4.2 and 4.3.)
- The use of evidence is generally good, particularly the inclusion of statistics (see section 8.2) in the third main section paragraph.
- The use of quotations throughout the essay is excessive. (See section 8.3.)
- The author has attempted to acknowledge their sources, but unfortunately the in-text citations are incorrectly formatted (see Chapter 10), due to incorrect secondary referencing (see section 5.3) and because the author has confused the editors with the authors of the cited chapters. (See Chapter 10.)
- The references in the reference list are mainly correctly formatted, but you will notice that they don't match the citations in the text. (See Chapter 10.)

Content

On this module, it is acceptable to use only the set text, audio and video materials. Consequently all of the references are from these. On a more advanced course it would be required to read Bauman in the original and the tutor would likely expect a longer set of 'outside' references.

Bauman's argument about consumer society and his core concepts of 'seduced' and 'repressed' are well drawn. Each of the claims is relevant to the topic and the range of claims and evidence demonstrates that the author understands a good breadth of supermarket power and consumer society issues.

You will have noticed, however, that the essay deviates slightly from the question: it begins and ends with the commonly accepted idea that supermarkets have actually expanded choice. The decision to include this bit of context was risky – the question doesn't ask for comparison – so do you think it was worth using 14 words on this? (I do, because I think it adds to the interest of the essay, but some tutors would consider it a waste of words.)

Social scientific skills

This is a real strength of the essay.

- As a whole, the essay answers the question as set. (See sections 2.3 and 4.2.)
- It does what an introductory level social science advocacy essay should do (see section 4.3): explores claims and the evidence for them. (See section 2.2.)
- The essay presents an appropriate series of 'claims', as one would expect from an 'outline' command (see section 4.2).
- Some of the claims are supported by quotations, working as evidence. (See section 8.3.) This could have worked much better, however, *if* the quotations had been consistently

attributed to their authors/cited authorities in the field. As it happens, John Allen and Georgina Blakeley are frequently attributed when in fact they are the *editors,* not the authors of the chapters being cited (Allen is the sole author of one chapter). (See Chapter 10.)

- Some of the claims are supported by evidence in the form of statistics. The Friends of the Earth statistics, as already noted, are well presented and support a couple of nicely nuanced claims. (See sections 2.2 and 8.2.)
- Quotations are over-used, in the sense that there are far too many of them, but there is a good selection and they are used correctly to illuminate an argument or support a point (or would have been had the author, rather than editors, been attributed). (See section 8.3.)
- There is a strong use of difficult key concepts, which are defined correctly and succinctly. (See sections 2.2 and 6.1.)
- While not always explicit, the student shows she or he is thinking like a social scientist (see section 2.2), particularly in the more complex paragraphs where different ideas are drawn together under a main theme, and in the appropriate selection of claims and evidence. (See section 3.3.)

Essay 4

Outline the argument that supermarket power constrains consumer choice.

In economically developed nations, such as the UK, supermarkets are commonly used to shop for various goods and are considered a convenient option for the consumer. I will be outlining the argument that supermarket power constrains consumer choice within the UK, looking at both 'market power' and 'positive-sum game'/'zero-sum game' concepts, using examples for and against with supporting evidence throughout. My conclusion will summarize the impact that supermarket chains have had on UK and wider society and how their presence may have caused certain constraints but also encouraged positive change overall.

Traditionally in the UK products were sold in smaller local stores along the high street, such as butchers, chemists, bakers etc., where consumers visited each store individually to purchase their goods, waiting their turn to be served by the shop assistant. Supermarkets were introduced in the UK during the 1960s and have influenced the behaviour of consumers in a huge way by offering a wider selection of goods all under one roof as opposed to having to shop in multiple stores on separate occasions. It is not only the consumer that has been affected by the many large supermarket chains that have come into play, the smaller local businesses and suppliers in the UK have also been put under pressure due to this new convenient way of shopping, along with the competitive prices and, more recently, online-to-doorstep services being offered too.

Firstly, I would like to look at what is called the 'market power' of the large supermarket chains, which demonstrates the power of a company to influence various conditions within the markets, e.g. price, quantities and promotional offerings. The market power of a supermarket can be extremely competitive due to the volume of goods ordered, which enables the large retailer to drive down pricing from wholesale suppliers. Local, smaller business, aren't able to order goods at the same volumes as supermarkets and are, therefore, unable to secure the same favourable deals, leading to higher prices being passed on to consumers. Where smaller retailers struggle to compete in this way, many are forced to close down. As a consequence, the large supermarket chains now tend to dominate local towns, and can be seen by some to limit and constrain the consumer by almost forcing them to shop at their stores. 'The big four supermarket chains – Tesco, Sainsbury's, Asda and Morrisons – take just over three out of every four pounds spent on groceries in the UK' (Kantar Worldwide, 2013).

Despite the pressure that supermarket retailers bring upon smaller retailers, they have also encouraged a wide number of positive changes in the UK too. For example, the diversity and choice of goods for the consumer has been significant and, despite the local businesses having to compete with these giants, it has provided an opportunity for them to look at ways in which they can offer and sell more 'boutique' items within their stores, which of course may not have been an option previously.

This leads me to my next point pertaining to supermarket chains in the UK. There are many situations where a 'zero-sum game' is presented. A zero-sum game is 'a situation in which one party's gain is balanced by another party's loss' (Allen and Blakeley, 2014, p. 158). Due to the supermarkets locating onto and nearby local high streets, some smaller businesses have been unable to compete and so have had to move elsewhere or simply close down. For example, Joanna Blythman explains, 'in the 1960s, there were ten bakers [in Dundee]; now there are two left. There were eight or nine butchers; now there is one. Of the five fishmongers, one has survived. Where there were half a dozen grocers, one remains' (Allen and Blakeley, 2014, p.163). By looking at the success of supermarkets and the financial impact on smaller local business, and consumer choices, we can see how unbalanced the situation is resulting in a zero-sum game outcome.

Conversely, there is a 'positive-sum game' scenario where both parties have equal gain. The buying power and global reach of the large supermarket chains mean that UK shoppers now have access to a diverse range of products that have been imported internationally, which prior to the 1960s was not as widely available. Due to the cheap labour opportunities from, for instance, textile companies in countries such as Bangladesh and India, the large retailers outsource their clothing requirements in order to gain a cheaper price for goods being produced. The wider choice in goods being offered by supermarkets, along with competitive pricing, has enabled consumers in the UK to shop in a more cost effective manner compared to previous years. The supermarkets have presented positive change in this respect, which in turn has also meant that they too have seen a significant rise in their revenue and business opportunities. Not only does this overseas opportunity benefit the supermarkets, and consumers, it creates employment opportunities for overseas textile workers.

On the other hand, in 2013 an incident occurred in Bangladesh at the Rana Plaza factory where over 1,100 workers making clothing for a large UK supermarket brand lost their lives due to a devastating fire in a garment factory (Open University, 2014). The cost of cheap clothing was a lack of safety provision for workers in the factory. Supermarkets and UK consumers have benefited from the cheap costs of garments being made overseas, but workers with poor working conditions have experienced devastating effects.

In conclusion, when looking at the constraints experienced by consumers in the UK, we can see both the positive and negative impact that supermarkets have had on consumer choice, as well as having wider social impacts. Despite the consumers' choices being restricted in terms of where they can shop locally with local stores being phased out over time, overall the benefits in cost-saving, the convenience of having everything in one store and access to a wider range of goods have demonstrated a positive change in the experience for the consumer overall. But it is important not to look at UK consumer choice in isolation, as the social and economic impacts of supermarket power reflect their global reach as well.

Word Count: 1021 words

References

Allen, J and Blakeley, G (2014, p. 158) 'Supermarket power: winners and losers' in 'Understanding Social Lives', Part 1, Milton Keynes, The Open University.

Joanna Blythman in Allen, J and Blakeley, G (2014, p. 163) 'Supermarket power: winners and losers' in 'Understanding Social Lives', Part 1, Milton Keynes, The Open University.

Kantar Worldwide (2013) Grocery Market Share UK (Online). Available at http://www.kantarworldpanel.com/en/grocery-market-share/great-britain (Accessed 10th December 2016)

Panorama: Dying for a Bargain (2013) BBC 1, 27 September (online). Available at https://learn2.open.ac.uk/mod/oucontent/view.php?id=698890&section=6 (Accessed 10 January 2016)

The Guardian 2007 'Supermarket power: winners and losers', in Allen, J & Blakeley, G (2014, p. 165) in Understanding Social Lives, Part 1, Milton Keynes, The Open University.

Commentary on Essay 4

You will probably notice that Essay 4 deals with the set topic, but does not follow the command. The author hasn't recognized that this is an advocacy question and that only the one argument (that supermarkets have constrained consumer choice), its claims and evidence, is required. There is a regular essay structure, and the essay is easy to follow. There is also some good discussion and convincing argument, albeit for the 'wrong' side. Some tutors would fail this essay, as it hasn't followed the core instruction. It does, however, have merit as a social science essay, has sections that work well (structurally and in terms of content) and is quite enjoyable to read.

Structure and writing skills

The essay has an introduction and a conclusion and a main body with some recognizable structure. There is some good use of social science vocabulary and terrific use of transitional words (see section 8.4) that help guide the reader from paragraph to paragraph:

- The introduction gives the context and sets parameters for the scope of the discussion (many people – in the UK – shop at supermarkets because they are convenient and offer lots of choice). It neatly restates the essay requirement and notes the key concepts that will be drawn upon. It tells the reader what the conclusion will do. There is plenty to recommend the introduction. (See Chapter 7.)
- The main body doesn't have an obvious, overall, logical structure related directly to the assignment. (See sections 3.1, 3.3 and 8.1.) There is some historical comparison, and there are a couple of attempts to put point and counter-point (which *is* logical), as well as to apply the concepts 'zero-sum game' and 'positive-sum game' to a consideration of the effects of supermarket power. (See sections 2.2 and 6.1.)
- The first main section paragraph provides historical background to shopping in the UK, comparing the 1960s with the present day. Although certainly interesting and well-described, this information wasn't asked for in the question. This paragraph uses 141 words – over 10 per cent of the allowed word count. (See sections 3.3, 3.4 and 8.1.)
- The second main section paragraph, which is concerned with market power, suggests in the first sentence (which defines market power) that it will cover 'price, quantity and promotional offerings'. While price and quantity are covered, promotional offerings are not. Nevertheless, the paragraph has done a good job of connecting supermarkets' behaviour in the wholesale market to impacts on smaller shops on the high street to consumer choice. (See section 8.1.)

- Paragraph three of the main section presents a counter-argument to the idea that super-market price competitiveness leads to smaller retailers closing.
- The next paragraph is an attempt to analyse the relationship between supermarkets and smaller retailers, in terms of the concept 'zero-sum game'. The quote from Joanna Blythman indicates the sorts of changes experienced on high streets between the 1960s and today. It doesn't, however, clearly connect the loss of independent bakers with the arrival of a supermarket. There may be an implied correlation but nothing more. (See section 8.1.)
- Following the zero-sum paragraph is a paragraph suggesting a positive-sum game results from supermarkets sourcing goods overseas from factories using low-waged labour, producing cheap goods. Consumers benefit from paying less for their shopping, while supermarkets improve their market share, and overseas workers gain employment.
- This is contrasted in the penultimate paragraph, which suggests supermarkets' overseas sourcing may not produce a positive outcome for all workers, as driving down costs may have led to poor working conditions and in turn to the Rana Plaza tragedy.
- The conclusion indicates that the student thought the assignment was a compare and contrast essay (see sections 2.3, 4.2 and 4.3), and that there was an expectation of evaluation.
- Throughout the essay, sentence structure is mostly very good, and in places quite sophisticated with, as noted above, some great use of transitional and conjunction words and phrases. (See sections 8.1 and 8.4.)
- Paragraphs benefit from the use of topic sentences; they mostly stay on track, and conclude with a clear statement. (See section 8.4.)
- The assignment doesn't ask for comparisons (historical or in terms of consumer choice benefits), but the essay is very concerned with comparisons. (See sections 2.3, 4.2 and 4.3.)
- The couple of quotations do good jobs of providing evidence for the claim posed. (See section 8.3.)
- More generally, though, there are too many claims that are not backed up by evidence whether in the form of statistics, the voice of authority, etc., and, relatedly, there are fewer citations than might be expected in an essay of this length. (See sections 6.2, 8.2 and 8.3.)
- The word count is somewhat low, and is outside the 10 per cent range of 1,250 words. (See sections 2.3 and 12.1.)

Content

The essay has relevance to the set assignment, but the student didn't read the assignment properly. As this was an advocacy question, the essay should have been concerned exclusively with claims allied to the idea that supermarket power constricts consumer choice. There are a number of ways in which this might have been explored, as demonstrated in Essay 3. The main relevant point raised (in a few different ways) in Essay 4 is that smaller, local retailers have closed; in some areas, the only consumer choice is between supermarket giants. Other ways in which consumer choice is constricted are only hinted at, or are implicit: most notably, the ethical issue of consumers with no choice but to buy from supermarkets which will source goods most cheaply, regardless of worker safety. The consideration of positive-sum and zero-sum concepts wasn't particularly helpful for the assignment as set, but did demonstrate the student's willingness to tackle tricky ideas in social science and, most admirably, to apply them to an example or specific context. While this is not a strong essay, it is one that shows promise.

Social scientific skills

There is a tendency in social science to want to 'jump in' with comparisons and evaluations and this is precisely the case here.

- While this suggests enthusiasm and interest in the topic and an eagerness to get on with 'doing' social science, it is important to remember how essential good description is to good social science. (See sections 2.2, 4.1 and 4.2.)
- Getting description right takes practice, and helping students with this will have been one of the objectives of setting this essay.
- Another objective, as discussed above, is making clear the connection between claims and evidence. Without evidence, a claim is unsubstantiated opinion. (See sections 2.2, 8.1 and 8.2.)
- Essay 4 includes some good evidence to back up some claims – and some really interesting discussion – but would have benefitted from a more rigorous, and simple, structure that attached evidence, and a citation to every claim. (See sections 8.1, 8.2 and 8.2.)
- The historical contextualization of the topic was not required, but it was interesting and for many other assignments, such context would be useful.
- Referencing is inaccurate and incomplete – both in-text and in the reference list. (See Chapter 10.)

Summary

- The material in this chapter illustrates stronger and weaker student essays.
- The strengths and weaknesses relate to: writing skills (such as the use of paragraphs and transitions) and essay structure; content; and social scientific skills (such as the use of description, theory and evidence).
- Analysing the essays and their accompanying commentary will help you identify what constitutes effective social scientific essay writing.

Self-test

1 What techniques of 'critical reading' might you use when reading the four student essays?
2 What elements of structure, content and style have you identified as being better/worse in each of the essays?
3 What is missing from each of the essays? (Answer: administrative requirements such as name, title page, etc.)

Don't forget! Visit **https://study.sagepub.com/redmanandmaples5** for more tasks and resources related to this chapter.

Appendix A

Editors' Symbols – Common Notations Made by Tutors

Ex.? or e.g.?	Include an example or illustration.
Gr.	Grammar is faulty.
i.e.?	Clarify
Incompl.	The sentence is incomplete – it may lack a verb or subject, or some other essential element. May also be used to indicate an incomplete argument or essay.
N.B.	'Note well', as in 'pay careful attention' (*nota bene*).
Ref. or cit.	A reference is required.
Run-on	The sentence amalgamates too many topics, or is actually two (or more) thoughts or sentences run together.
Punc.	Punctuation is faulty.
Sp.	Spelling is incorrect.
w/c	Word choice. Indicates that the tutor is not sure you have said what you mean – or perhaps thinks you have misunderstood a term. Suggests there is a more appropriate or accurate word.
✓	Can mean: 'I have read this bit', 'Good' or 'Correct' – you may wish to clarify this with your tutor.
✗	Incorrect.

(Continued)

Appendix A   (Continued)

λ	Insert here. Often used when there is a note in the margin. This symbol indicates where in the text an additional or replacement word, phrase, example, etc., might be inserted.
≈	Approximately the same, but not quite. Can be used when an example doesn't actually support an argument, or when a translation of an argument isn't quite right.
≠	Not the same.
¶	Requires a new paragraph.
~~Your words~~	A line through your words could mean that they are superfluous to the sentence or paragraph, or that they are incorrect. If you are not sure, ask your tutor.
Words your	The wavy line suggests swapping the words, sentence or paragraph around, in this case to read 'Your words'.

Appendix B
Abbreviations and Words in Foreign Languages

At various points in your reading, especially in references, you will come across various abbreviations or words written in foreign languages. You may need to use these in your own writing, so here's a list of some of the more common examples.

cf. (*confer*)	compare
ch., chs (or chap., chaps)	chapter(s)
ed., eds	editor(s)
edn	edition
e.g. (*exempli gratia*)	'for example' (not to be confused with 'i.e.'). Used when an actual example is given, as in the following: 'Some forms of analysis (e.g. Marxist and feminist theories) suggest that social phenomena are the product of underlying and prior social divisions.'
et al. (*et aliia*)	'and others', used to indicate multiple authors or editors, as in '(Bingham et al., 2013)'
et seq. (*et sequens*)	'and the following' (for example, pp. 16 et seq.)
etc. (*et cetera*)	'and the rest'/'and so on'
ff. (*folio*)	alternative to et seq. (for example, pp. 16 ff.)

(Continued)

Appendix B   (Continued)

ibid. (*ibidem*)	'in the same work' (as the last reference). Used in footnotes/endnotes to save writing out the whole reference again (for example, 'Ibid. p. 61')
i.e. (*id est*)	'that is' (not to be confused with 'e.g.'). Used to explain, define or clarify as in the following: 'Radical feminists (i.e. feminists who maintain that gender relations are the product of a universal and unitary system of male dominance) argue that …'
loc. cit. (*loco citato*)	'in the same place' (as the previous passage)
n., nn.	note(s), as in 'p. 4, n. 2'
op. cit. (*opere citato*)	'in the work recently cited' as in 'Gilroy, op. cit., p. 67'; used in footnotes/endnotes to save writing a full reference for a work previously cited, but not the last reference (cf. 'ibid.')
p., pp.	page, pages
passim	throughout the work (not on one page only)
q.v. (*quod vide*)	'which see' (for cross-referencing)
(sic)	'thus'; indicates that questionable/apparently incorrect quoted material is faithfully reproduced from the original
trans., tr.	translator
vol., vols	volume(s)

References

Andrews, G. (2005) 'Dissent and the re-invention of politics', in Andrews, G. and Saward, M. (eds), *Living Political Ideas*, Edinburgh, Edinburgh University Press/ The Open University.

Bilić, P. (2015) '"Searching for a centre that holds" in the network society: Social construction of knowledge on, and with, English Wikipedia', in *New Media and Society*, vol. 17, no. 8, pp. 1258–1276. Available at: http://nms.sagepub.com.libez proxy.open.ac.uk/content/17/8/1258.full.pdf+html, DOI: 10.1177/1461444814522953 (Accessed 29 May 2016).

Bolton, G. (2014) *Reflective Practice*, 4th edn., London, Sage.

BPS (1994) *Guidelines for External Examiners on Undergraduate Psychology Degrees*, Leicester, British Psychological Society/Association of Heads of Psychology Departments.

Burns, T. and Sinfield, S. (2008) *Essential Study Skills: The Complete Guide to Success at University*, 2nd edn., London, Sage.

Coats, M. (undated) *Open Teaching Toolkit: Learning How to Learn*, Milton Keynes, The Open University.

Cole, S. and Harris, P. (undated) *Open Teaching Toolkit: Revision and Examinations*, Milton Keynes, The Open University.

Dorling, D. (2014) *Inequality and the 1%*, London, Verso.

FIFA (2014) FIFA World Cup Brazil Image Archive [Online]. Available at: www.fifa.com/worldcup/archive/brazil2014/index.html (Accessed 29 May 2016).

Foreign and Commonwealth Office (2016) Foreign travel advice: Egypt [Online]. Available at: www.gov.uk/foreign-travel-advice/egypt (Accessed 29 May 2016).

Hall, S. (1992) 'The question of cultural identity', in S. Hall, D. Held and A. McGrew (eds), *Modernity and its Futures*, Cambridge, Polity Press, in association with the Open University.

Hall, S. (1997) *Representation: Cultural Representations and Signifying Practices*. London, Sage, in association with the Open University.

Headlee, C. (2016) '10 ways to have a better conversation', TED Talks, posted February 2016 at: www.ted.com/talks/celeste_headlee_10_ways_to_have_a_better_conversation (accessed 25 May 2016).

MacKay, H. and Reynolds, P. (2001) 'Social science and making sense of the information society', in MacKay, H., Maples, W. and Reynolds, P. (eds), *Social Science in Action: Investigating the Information Society*, Milton Keynes, The Open University.

Nash, K. (2009) 'Between citizenship and human rights', in *Sociology*, vol. 43, no. 6, pp. 1067–1083.

Office for National Statistics (2016a) 'Visits abroad by UK residents', Table 6.02 [Online]. Available at: www.ons.gov.uk/peoplepopulationandcommunity/leisure andtourism/datasets/overseastravelandtourism (Accessed 28 May 2016).

Office for National Statistics (2016b) 'UK visits abroad: All visits', Table 2.10 [Online]. Available at: www.ons.gov.uk/peoplepopulationandcommunity/leisure andtourism/timeseries/gmax/linechartimage?series=&fromMonth=01&fromYear =1986&toMonth=12&toYear=2016&frequency=months (Accessed 28 May 2016).

Office for National Statistics (2016c) 'Number of visits abroad: by main country visited 2011–2015', Table 3.10 [Online]. Available at: www.ons.gov.uk/people populationandcommunity/leisureandtourism/datasets/ukresidentsvisitsabroad (Accessed 23 September, 2016).

Office for National Statistics (2016d) 'Visits to the UK by overseas residents, 2006–2015', Table 1 [Online]. Available at: www.ons.gov.uk/peoplepopulationandcommunity/lei sureandtourism/datasets/overseastravelandtourism/current (Accessed 24 September 2016).

Osborne, R. and Brew, A. (2016) *Sociology for Beginners*, London, Zidane.

Poore, M. (2014) *Studying and Researching with Social Media*, London, Sage.

Redman, P. (2002) 'Writing in your own words', Milton Keynes, The Open University.

Rubin, D. (1983) *Teaching Reading and Study Skills in Content Areas*, London, Holt, Reinhart and Winston.

Schirato, T., Danaher, G. and Webb, J. (2012) *Understanding Foucault: A Critical Introduction*, London, Sage.

Seely, J. (2013) *The Oxford A–Z of Grammar and Punctuation*, 2nd edn., Oxford, Oxford University Press.

Sherratt, N., Goldblatt, D., Mackintosh, M. and Woodward, K. (2000) DD100 *An Introduction to the Social Sciences: Understanding Social Change, Workbook 1*, Milton Keynes, The Open University.

Taylor, A. (2003) 'Trading with the environment', in Bingham, N., Blowers, A. and Belshaw, C. (eds), *Contested Environments*, Chichester/Milton Keynes, Wiley/The Open University.

Truss, L. (2009) *Eats, Shoots and Leaves: The Zero Tolerance Approach to Punctuation*, London, HarperCollins.

Index

Page numbers in *italics* refer to figures

abbreviated references 102–3, 105, 107–18
abbreviations 175–6
abstracts 61
academic convention, referencing as 100–1, 121–2
academic writing 121–2
active reading 41–5
administrative requirements 22
advanced level
  audience 87–8
  conclusions 96, 144
  introductions 62, 66–7, 143
  question formulation 59–60
  question type
    advocacy questions 33
    compare and contrast questions 34–5
    evaluation questions 36
  selecting evidence 72–3, 84
  using theory 81–2
  writing skills 143–4
advice 4 *see also* guidance notes
advocacy questions 31–3
Andrews, Geoff 90–3
arguments
  adding weight to 84–7
  being self-reflexive 83
  communicating 87–93
  conclusions 95–8
  establishing a position 65
  example essays 153, 165
  formulating 58–60
  introductions 62–6, 65
  referencing 99–100
  signposting 63–4, 65, 66, 91–2
  structuring 69–72
  supporting evidence 72–84
articles, referencing 108–9
audience 87–8
audio-visual material, referencing 112–14, 116

authors
  quoted in another text 116
  referencing films 112–14
  referencing multiple authors 106, 108
  referencing organizations 111–12
  referencing single authors 102–4, 105
autobiography 129

bad fail *138*, 140
bare fail *138*, 139–40
bare pass *138*, 139, 139–40
bias and subjectivity 83, 128–9
bibliographies 100 *see also* reference lists
Bilić, Paško 85–7
blogs 53
  referencing 110
Bolton, Gillie 124
bookmarking websites 49, 53
books
  abbreviated references 102–3, 104
  eBooks 105–7
  edition numbers 105, 117–18
  multiple authors 106, 108
  publication dates 117–18
  referencing 102–8
  single author 102–4, 105
bullet points 123
Burns, Tom 41–3, 50–1

causation 76
circuit of social scientific knowledge 7–10, *8*, *9*, 55, 56, 59–60, 163
citations 48 *see also* quotations; references, abbreviated
  defining 99–100
  example essays 165, 171
  styles of 101
claims 7–10, 57, 123
  example essays 165–6, 169, 170, 171
clear fail *138*, 140

clear pass *138*, 139
close reading 41–5
Coats, Maggie 16–17
cognitive skills 25–31, 59–60
coherence 57
Cole, Sue 26–31
collaborative publishing 118
command words 25–31
compare and contrast questions 33–5, 170
comprehensiveness 57
computer research *see* online sources
computer software
    for note-taking 48
    for referencing 101, 119
    for wordstorming 18, *19*
conclusions 7, 95–8
    advanced writing skills 96, 144
    advocacy questions 32–3
    compare and contrast questions 34
    evaluation questions 36
    example essays 154, 159, 164, 170
    intermediate writing skills 142
    introductory writing skills 95–6, 141
conference papers, referencing 112
confidence and plagiarism 131
content, example essays 154, 159, 165,
    170–1
content words 25, 40
contested terms 64
convention (academic) 100–1, 121–2
core materials 50
    reading lists 49
correlation 76
course requirements, grade bands 137–8
credibility of sources 51
critical approach to data 81–2
critical approach to reading 41–5, 55–6
critical approach to theory 81–2
critical thinking 55–7
current affairs, selecting evidence 73

data *see also* literature searches
    critical approach to 81–2
    gathering 51–3
    primary data 52
    secondary data 51
    selecting evidence 74–80
debates
    compare and contrast questions 34
    errors in essays 10–11
    example essays 153, 159, 164–5
    in introductions 63–4, 66
defining terms, in introductions 64, 66
description 26
    example essays 171

diagrams
    referencing 101
    selecting evidence 74–80
directions 89–90 *see also* signposting
discussion 28–9
drafts 21–2, 22–3
DVDs, referencing 113

eBooks, referencing 105–7
edited collections, referencing 107
edition numbers 105, 117–18
editors' symbols 173–4
electronic sources *see* DVDs, referencing;
        films; online sources; podcasts; television
        programmes
empirical data 51–2
empirical evidence 74
epistemology 7–10
essay plans 18–21
essays 121–2
    common errors 10–12
    examples 146–71
    features of social science essays 7–10
    golden rules 12
    reflective 123–4, 128–9
    structure 6–7, 11
establishing a position 65
'et al.' 107
evaluation 29–30
    errors in essays 10–11
    example essays 153, 155, 159
    as a feature of social science essays 7–10
evaluation questions 35–6
evidence
    being 'critical' 81–2
    empirical 74
    errors in essays 10–11
    example essays 153, 154, 159, 164, 165, 166,
        170, 171
    examples 72–3
    as a feature of reflective essays 124
    as a feature of report writing 123
    as a feature of social science essays 7–10
    as a feature of wikis 125
    judging 56–7
    in main sections 72–84
    maps, diagrams and numerical data 74–80
    using theories 81–2
exam writing 125–6
example essays 146–71
examples, selecting evidence 72–3
excellent pass 137–8, *138*
executive summaries 123
experience, personal 129, 160
explanation 29

fail grades *138*, 139–40
feedback 16–18
films, referencing 112–14
final drafts 21–2
first drafts 21–2, 23
first person 124, 128–9
flow of essay 92–3
foreign language terms 175–6
forums, referencing 115
full introductions 62–6

Goldblatt, David 57
golden rules 12
good pass *138*, 138–9
government publications, referencing 110–11
grades 137–8
    marking schemes 137–40
grammar 22, 129–30
    common errors 11–12
    example essays 159, 164, 170
graphics *see* data; diagrams; maps
guidance notes 15–16, 22

Hall, Stuart 58, 82
Harris, Pauline 26–31
Harvard referencing system
    advanced 115–18
    basic conventions 104
    basic principles 101–15
headings and subheadings 123
hyperlinks 48
hypotheses *see* claims

'I', use of 124, 128–9
index cards 46, 48
index searches 40
information, sources of 50–1 *see also* literature
    searches
intermediate level
    conclusions 142
    introductions 66–7, 142
    question formulation 59–60
    question types
        advocacy questions 33
        compare and contrast questions 34–5
        evaluation questions 36
    selecting evidence 72–3
    using theory 81–2
    writing skills 142–3
internet sources 52–3 *see also* online sources
interpretation 27–8
introductions 6, 61–7
    advanced level 62, 66–7, 143
    advocacy questions 32
    compare and contrast questions 33

introductions *cont.*
    evaluation questions 35
    example essays 154, 159, 163–4, 169
    intermediate writing skills 66–7, 142
    introductory writing skills 62, 66–7, 141
    long 62–6
    short 66–7
    when to write 67
introductory level
    conclusions 95–6, 141
    introductions 62, 66–7, 141
    question formulation 59–60
    question types
        advocacy questions 33
        compare and contrast questions 34–5
        evaluation questions 36
    writing skills 141
introductory points 90
italic type 104
iTunes, referencing 114

jargon 88, 129–30
journalistic writing 122–3
journals, referencing 108–9

key concepts 64
key debates *see* major debates
key skills 136–7
key words 40, 48
key works, adding weight to your argument
    84–7
knowledge 7–10

language *see also* terminology
    academic 88–9
    and flow of essay 92–3
    foreign terms 175–6
    technical 64, 88–9, 130–1
    using 'I' 124, 128–9
learning guides, referencing 116
learning outcomes 136–7
length
    of conclusion 95
    of essay 12, 16, 127–8
        example essays 154, 159, 165, 170
    of introduction 61–2
levels
    audience 87–8
    conclusions 95–6, 141, 144
    introductions 62, 66–7, 141, 143
    main sections 141, 142, 143
    question formulation 59–60
    question types
        advocacy questions 33
        compare and contrast questions 33–5

levels *cont.*
    evaluation questions 36
    selecting evidence 72–3, 84
    using theory 81–2
    writing skills 140–4
libraries 50
linear notes 19, *21*, 46
link words *see* transition words and phrases
list of references *see* reference lists
literature reviews 125
literature searches 49–53
logical progression
    example essays 154, 159, 165
    preparation 18
    structuring arguments 69–72, *71*

MacKay, Hugh 56, 57
main sections 6
    adding weight to your argument 84–7
    advanced writing skills 143
    advocacy questions 32
    communicating your argument 87–93
    compare and contrast questions 33–4
    evaluation questions 35–6
    giving direction 89–90
    intermediate writing skills 142
    introductory writing skills 141
    making your essay flow 92–3
    structure 69–72
    using evidence 72–84
major debates
    compare and contrast questions 34
    errors in essays 10–11
    example essays 154, 159, 164–5
    in introductions 63–4, 66
maps
    referencing 101
    selecting evidence 74–80
margin notes 45, 48
marking essays 137–40
    marking schemes 137–40
    tutor notations 173–4
    writing skills 140–4
marking up textbooks 45
material, preparation 18–21
memory retention 45, 48
mindmaps 18, *20*, 46, *47*

Nash, Kate 43–4
news articles 122–3
news sources, selecting evidence 73
newspaper articles, referencing 109–10
non-governmental organization publications
    111–12
notebooks 19, 46

note-taking 45–8, 56
    computer software for 48
    linear notes 19, *21*, 46
    margin notes 45, 48
    plagiarism 48, 131
numerical data
    referencing 101
    selecting evidence 74–80

objectivity 83, 128–9
official publications, referencing 110–11
online books, referencing 105–7
online sources
    bookmarking 49, 53
    referencing 109, 110, 111, 112, 114, 115
online support 4–5, 53, 101
organization publications, referencing 111–12

paragraphs 88–9, 92–3
paraphrasing 130–1
pass requirements, grade bands 137–40
peer group learning 53
peer review 51, 52
peers, essays checked by 130
periodicals, referencing 108–9
personal communications, referencing 117
plagiarism 130–1, 134
    common errors in essays 11, 130–4
    example essays 159
    and internet 52
    and note-taking 48, 131
    reasons for references 100
plans 18–21
podcasts, referencing 114
preparation 14–23
presentation 129–30
primary data 52
process words 25–31
publication dates 117–18
publishers, referencing 118
punctuation 129–30
    common errors in essays 11–12
    example essays 159, 165
purposeful reading 38–45

questions
    command words in 25–31
    compare and contrast questions 170
    errors in essays 10–11
    example essays 165
    as feature of social science essays 7–10
    formulating 59–60
    in full introductions 62
    preparation 15–16, 21
    reading and unpacking 24–5

questions *cont.*
   types of
      advocacy 31–3
      compare and contrast 33–5
      evaluation 35–6
quotation marks 104, 131
quotations
   adding weight to your argument 84–7
   author quoted in another text 116
   example essays 154, 159, 163–4, 165–6, 170
   plagiarism 130–1
   referencing 87, 101, 102–3

reading 38–45
   active reading 41–5
   close reading 41–5
   critical approach to 41–5, 55–6
   purposeful reading 38–45
   skim reading 39–41
reading lists 49
recapping 91–2, 95–6, 97
reference lists 7, 22, 48, 100, 103–4
references, abbreviated
   author quoted in another text 116
   books 102–3, 104
   edited collections 107
   film, television and DVD 112–14
   Government/official publications 110–11
   journals/periodicals 108–9
   multiple authors 106, 108
   newspapers 109
   non-governmental organization publications
      111–12
   online sources 110, 111
   personal communication 117
   retaining early publication dates 117
references, full
   author quoted in another text 115–16
   books 103–4
   conference papers 112
   defining 99–100
   eBooks 106–7
   edited collections 107
   editions 117–18
   film and television 112–14
   government/official publications 110–11
   journals/newspapers 108–9
   non-governmental organization publications
      111–12
   online books 105–7
   online sources 109, 110, 111, 112, 114, 115
   personal communications 117
referencing
   and academic convention 100–1, 121–2
   advanced 115–18

referencing *cont.*
   basic principles 101–15
   compiling 118–19
   dates and international conventions 109
   defining 99–100
   example essays 154, 159, 165, 170, 171
   finding details for 102
   maps, diagrams and numerical data 101
   publishing details 117–18
   quotations 87, 101, 102–3
   reasons for 100–1
   retaining early publication dates 117
   secondary referencing 115–16
referencing tools 49, 101, 118–19
reflective essays 123–4, 128–9
reliability 56–7
report writing 123
research *see also* literature searches
   example essays 154
   as a feature of social science essays 7–8
   selecting evidence 72–3
research projects 125
Reynolds, Paul 56
Rubin method 89

Sarre, Phil 26–31
search engines 53
secondary data 51
secondary referencing 115–16
selectivity 19, 45, 72–3
self-reflection 128–9
self-reflexivity 83, 124
sentences 88–9, 92–3
Sherratt, N, *8, 9*
short introductions 66–7
signposting 91–2
   example essays 154, 159, 164
   full introductions 63–4, 65–6
   short introductions 66–7
Sinfield, Sandra 41–3, 50–1
skills *see* cognitive skills; key skills; social
      scientific skills; writing skills
skim reading 39–41
social scientific skills 11
   example essays 154–5, 159–60, 165–6, 171
software *see* computer software
sources *see also* citations; referencing
   credibility 51, 52
   defining 100
   empirical evidence 74
   maps, diagrams and numerical data
      74–80
   preparation 18–21
   selecting evidence 72–3
spell check 22

spelling 129–30
    common errors in essays 11–12
    example essays 159, 165
stages of writing 14
    drafts 21–2, 23
    introduction 61–7
    plan 18–21
    question and guidance 15–16
    time management 22–3
standards, grade bands 137–40
structure
    of essays 6–7, 11
    example essays 154, 158–9, 163–5, 169–70
    given in introductions 65–6
    main sections 69–72
    of news articles 122–3
    of reflective essays 124
    of reports 123
    of wikis 125
subject benchmarks 136–7
subjectivity and bias 83, 128–9
subjects
    choosing 58–9
    in introductions 62, 66–7
    referring back to 92
summaries
    example essays 155, 164
    giving direction 90
    note-taking 45
    recapping 91–2
    writing in your own words 131–4
summary questions 27
synopsis, introduction as 61

Taylor, Annie 39, 40–1
technical language 64, 88–9, 130–1
television programmes, referencing 112–14
terminology 64, 88–9, 130–1, 155, 160
    foreign language words 175–6
    jargon 88, 129–30
textbooks 50
    marking up 45
theory
    common errors in essays 11
    critical approach 81–2
    defining terms 64

theory *cont.*
    and evaluation 36, 83
    example essays 155, 159, 164
    as a feature of social science essays 8–10
    selecting evidence 81–2
    writing from 'within' 82–3
time management 22–3
titles 6, 92
topics *see* subjects
transition words and phrases 92–3, 170
tutors *see* marking essays

underlining 104
understanding and plagiarism 131, 134
university libraries 50
URLs 109, 116

validity 56
VLE (virtual learning environments) 53
vocabulary 64, 88–9, 130–1, 155, 160
voice 121, 134

websites *see* online sources
Weedon, Chris 116
Wetherell, Margaret 82
Wikipedia 49, 52, 85–7, 124–5, 131
wikis 86–7
    writing 124–5
word limits 12, 16, 61–2, 95, 127–8
    example essays 155, 165, 170
wordstorming 18, *19*
writing, types of 122–3
writing in your own words 11, 48, 131–4
    note-taking 45–8, 56, 131
writing skills
    academic writing 121–2
    advanced level 143–4
    essay-marking 140–4
    exam writing 125–6
    example essays 153–5, 158–9, 163–5, 169–70
    intermediate level 142–3
    introductory level 141
    reflective writing 123–4, 128–9
writing style 88–9

YouTube, referencing 114–15